*An Introduction to
the Art Song*

By the same author

Nineteenth-century French Song:
Fauré, Duparc, Chausson, Debussy

An Introduction to the Art Song

by Barbara Meister

A CRESCENDO BOOK
TAPLINGER PUBLISHING COMPANY
New York

First edition

Published in 1980 by
TAPLINGER PUBLISHING CO., INC.
New York, New York

Copyright © 1980 by Barbara Meister

Library of Congress Cataloging in Publication Data

Meister, Barbara
  An introduction to the art song.

  Includes index.
  1. Songs—History and criticism.   I. Title.
ML2800.M44 1980   784'.3   79-66640
ISBN 0-8008-8032-3

designed by Jim Harris

To my Parents

Acknowledgments

I should like to thank the staff of Lincoln Center Library, headed by David Hall (Record Archives) and Jean Bloch (Music Research), for their patience and expertise. I should also like to express gratitude to friend and cohort Abba Bogin for his valuable suggestions and corrections. Special thanks too to Matthew Meister for his help in compiling the Index and Glossary of Musical Terms.

Contents

Introduction	11
Historical Background	18
Early Italian Songs	23
Henry Purcell	26
Georg Friedrich Händel and Johann Sebastian Bach	28
Franz Joseph Haydn	34
Wolfgang Amadeus Mozart	40
Ludwig van Beethoven	48
Lesser Known German Composers Before Schubert	55
Franz Schubert	58
Robert Schumann	71
Felix Mendelssohn	80
Johannes Brahms	84
Hugo Wolf	92
Gustav Mahler and Richard Strauss	102
Arnold Schoenberg and Alban Berg	110
Hector Berlioz, Charles Gounod, César Franck, and Georges Bizet	120
Gabriel Fauré	126
Ernest Chausson and Henri Duparc	133
Claude Debussy	141
Maurice Ravel, Erik Satie, Darius Milhaud, and Francis Poulenc	149
Nationalism, Part I: The Russians	158
Nationalism, Part II: Spain, Norway, Bohemia, Finland, and Denmark	172

Contemporary England and the U.S.A.   182
Interpretation   193
Glossary of Musical Terms   199
Index   205

Introduction

What's in a name? Nothing intimidates the layman more than esoteric terminology. In any field special use of language—jargon, if you will—while allowing the initiated to communicate with one another in a useful verbal shorthand, confuses those not privy to the code words.

In music the issue is complicated by the fact that some terms are almost always used in Italian regardless of the home language while others are derived from Greek or German. Furthermore, many musical terms have changed their meanings over the years. The word sonata, now usually used to describe a composition for solo instrument or pair of instruments consisting of two or more contrasting movements of which at least one is in sonata form,* originally meant any instrumental piece, as opposed to cantata, any vocal work. By the seventeenth century the word cantata had also developed a more specific meaning, and today we associate the cantata with Protestant church music. Similarly the word tenor, now commonly used to designate the highest natural male voice other than the countertenor, once referred to the voice holding the long thematic notes (from the Latin *tenere,* "to hold") in part songs. Since these thematic notes were most often in the lowest registers, the tenor voice was on the bottom, not on the top.

---

*Sonata form is a specific structure involving an exposition, development, and recapitulation, with a prescribed set of harmonic relationships, which is usually used for the first movement of a symphony, concerto, quartet, trio, or sonata.

Similar linguistic difficulties arise in discussions of the serious classical song. In English and French the German word lied (lieder in the plural) indicates a song by a classical composer suitable for inclusion in a formal recital by a professional artist with a trained voice. The song may be in any language but it must be "classical." In Germany, however, lied simply means song, whether it is popular or classical, although younger people use the English word "song" when referring to American-style rock and disco numbers. In French common parlance chanson means song, the songs of Edith Piaf or Yves Montand, for instance, but for the French musicologist the chanson is a specific kind of polyphonic (many-voiced) song found in abundance in the Middle Ages. To avoid confusion (!) the term mélodie has been substituted when classical songs are under discussion, but since this word still means tune or melody whether sung or played on an instrument, who's to say which is more confusing? In this work we shall refer to serious songs of all nations, in all languages, as art songs.

There are three ways to publish an art song: as a single unit, as one of several separate songs grouped under a single opus number, and as part of a song cycle. The difference between the two latter schemes is obvious—in a true cycle there must be continuity of textual subject matter (the poems are usually by one author) and smooth harmonic transitions from one song to the next. Often musical material from the first song will be reiterated in the last, giving a truly cyclical effect. In a successful cycle the whole is much more than a sum of its parts and the composer is done a serious disservice if the integrity of the work is violated. None of this is true when a publisher merely groups a handful of songs under one opus number for his and the buyer's convenience.

When is a song an art song? When the singer brays through his nasal passages with the aid of thousands of kilowatts of electricity, the cacophonous accompaniment consists of one endlessly repeated chord progression, and the lyrics approximate "You Ain't Nothing but a Tugboat," there is no doubt that we are not hearing an art song. When an innocent voice charms us with a naive rendition of "On Top of Old Smokey," we have no trouble identifying folk song. The "Bell Song" from *Lakmé,* with its coloratura acrobatics, is obviously an operatic aria, and though we may thrill to its virtuosic display, we still do not mistake it for an art song. What then are the characteristics of this particular form of music?

First there is a degree of intimacy that is seldom equaled in other kinds of music, for the singer and accompanist, with a minimum of extramusical gesture, must communicate to the audience the most subtle and evanescent emotions as expressed in the poem and music. For this reason large halls are not the best settings for art song recitals, although a few major artists can overcome cavernous surroundings through the sheer intensity of their personalities.

Second, there is a partnership between singer and accompaniment that makes of the art song the most sensitive type of collaboration. In the greatest examples of the form, the piano parts are as expressive as the vocal parts, often conveying in music essential elements of the poems' meanings with more immediacy than the words themselves. In these cases the word "accompaniment" is an unfortunate misnomer.

The bulk of the art song literature is composed for a solo singer with piano. In vocal chamber-music, a variety of art song, we may have other instruments joining the pianist, or a combination of voices and instrumentation. Schubert's "Der

Hirt auf dem Felsen" features a clarinet obbligato; Ravel's *Chansons Madécasses* calls for flute, cello, piano, and voice; Brahms's *Liebeslieder Waltzes* are composed for a quartet of singers—soprano, alto, tenor, bass—and two players at one piano. There is also a fairly extensive body of work for voice and orchestra such as Mahler's *Lieder eines fahrenden Gesellen,* which is really a song cycle with a symphonic setting.

In most art songs the quality of the poem or text is of the utmost importance, although there are a few vocalises (wordless vocal parts) of great beauty by such composers as Rachmaninov, Ravel, and Ralph Vaughan Williams. The texts certainly need not be solemn—Leonard Bernstein has set recipes and riddles to music—but they must be treated seriously even if as high comedy. Above all they must be understood, and conscientious singers do their best to make this possible. No song recital program is complete without translations of the foreign texts; singers should enlighten audiences with a précis before each song if no written translation is given.

An art song is usually a self-contained unit. Arias or songs excerpted from opera or musical comedy scores are not really in this domain, although there are exceptions and borderline cases. This is not an arbitrary distinction, for a composer is very much influenced by whether he has three minutes or three hours in which to make his point.

There is a close kinship between one type of art song and folk song, the only clear-cut distinction being that the art song is composed by one specific person while the folk song is usually the result of traditions and accretions. Many examples exist of folk songs set to piano accompaniments by classical composers—Brahms, Ravel, and Benjamin Britten have been especially successful in this hybrid medium—and one finds even more numerous instances of composers incorporating folk material in original pieces. Needless to say the majority of art songs do not resemble folk song, nor do all folk songs respond to classical treatment.

Although effective rendition of an art song requires great skill on the part of the singer, virtuosity for its own sake is generally eschewed. Hence one seldom finds florid passages or excessive ornamentation. This is especially true of the French art song where declamatory vocal lines abound, and is due in part to the emphasis placed on the words, which tend to become obscured in fioritura writing. This characteristic also distinguishes art song from most operatic arias.

In the twentieth century, wild melodic leaps and improbable melodic intervals have become commonplace, removing the contemporary art song from the grasp of even the more talented amateurs. This is a pity, for with the piano duet, the art song has long been among the favorite outlets for the serious and skilled nonprofessional music lover.

There are basically two types of art song, the strophic, in which all the poem's verses are sung to the same music, and the through-composed, where each section of the text receives fresh music. Folk songs are usually strophic, and art songs based on folk material are often in that form. If any one piece of music is to be appropriate for several stanzas of verse, it must of necessity be fairly simple and nonevocative; only a text of similar naiveté can be properly served by a strophic setting. There are exceptional cases in which the musical repetition provides dramatic irony for the changing text, or where an almost hypnotic monotony is desired.

There will, of course, be some repetition in a through-composed song, which may take the simple ABA form or some variety thereof. Since no one type of poetry dominates the art song, there can be no pat formula for the music, which must follow the metrical arrangement, rhyme scheme, and overall structure of the text.

One of the things which most clearly distinguishes art songs from even the finest popular ballads is structure. The music of the vast majority of popular songs is confined to an eight-bar phrase which is repeated note for note, an eight-bar "bridge" or contrasting section, and a final repeat of the original eight bars. Even when the eight-bar phrase is extended to nine or ten measures, the basic AABA form prevails. This rigid repetition makes the popular song easier to recognize and remember, but severely limits the text and robs the songs of spontaneity and artistic development. Nevertheless it is certainly true that the best of the popular songwriters have occasionally risen above the limitations of the form to compose pieces of considerable inspiration. Sometimes, when writing for the musical theater, such composers as Jerome Kern, George Gershwin, Cole Porter, and Frank Loesser abandoned the format altogether, and many of their more serious efforts deserve a place in the art song repertoire.

In contrast to the regular 3/4 or 4/4 beats of most popular songs, many twentieth-century art songs feature enormous rhythmic freedom and complexity. Progressive jazz places considerable emphasis on complex rhythms too, but seldom in the service of vocal numbers. Even when vocal jazz rhythms are highly complex and improvisational, the steady background 4/4 beat that is the signature of jazz creates an aura quite different from that of the art song.

In instrumental classical music, if a piece is written in a particular key, it is always performed in that key. Beethoven's First Symphony is in C Major, his fifth in C Minor for now and forever more! In fact some composers find special significance in keys, and invariably choose one for drama, one for gaiety, and so forth.

In vocal music all this is tempered by the variety of vocal ranges and the obvious limitations of any one human voice.

Thus we may find a particular song published for high (tenor or soprano), medium (baritone or mezzo-soprano), or low (bass or alto) voice. Obviously the composer chose one of those ranges for his original rendering of the song, and the others are transpositions.

It is very simple to transpose a song with piano accompaniment, but altering the key of a piece of vocal chamber-music or—worse—a song with symphonic setting, presents many difficulties. Do we thus exceed the range of the instruments involved? Must we now give the oboe solo to a flute? Despite problems and expenses, some symphonic songs (and for that matter operatic arias) are transposed. Compromises are sometimes effected—a single unusual high note replaced with an alternate suggested, if necessary, by the composer (marked ossia), for instance.

In the following text, songs are discussed in their original keys unless otherwise specified.

It has often been said that the better the poem, the less need it has for a musical setting, that the greatest poems make the least successful songs because the composer can add nothing. While it is true that putting Hamlet's Soliloquy to music seems like a pretty poor idea, some very fine poems have inspired marvelous songs. On the other hand, many mediocre texts have been infused with greatness by first-rate settings. The converse does not seem to hold—the finest verse cannot rescue banal music from its deficiencies.

What do composers seek in a text? Words that have a melodious quality of their own, words that evoke definite moods, words that flow rhythmically, and above all words that release the musical inspiration within them.

Historical Background

Ever since the discovery of the animal figures painted by Cro-Magnon man some twenty thousand to thirty thousand years ago in caves throughout southern France and northern Spain, we have acknowledged artistic creativity to be a feature of even the most primitive human societies. Recent discoveries of equally ancient musical instruments—six-hole flutes carved out of bone or ivory, pitched percussion sets, whistles—confirm assumptions that prehistoric man enjoyed music as well as art. The awesome cave drawings are there for all to see; the music can only be imagined.

There are three basic elements in the music of Western civilization: melody, rhythm, and harmony. Nature provides models for all but the last, and we can assume that primitive man employed the first and second, imitating the melodic warbling of the birds and the rhythmic beat of his own pulse.

It would not be surprising if song and speech developed almost simultaneously, for even animals use rising and falling pitch-levels in mating calls and other forms of communication. The natural differences in vocal range between male and female or adult and child must have provided added stimulus for the development of an awareness of the possibilities of deliberately varied pitches, or melodic lines.

Unfortunately for music historians, musical notation developed rather late, and we have yet to decipher with certainty its earliest forms. Hence although we know from written reports that music played an important part in Greek drama, we cannot be sure of all the sounds indicated by neumes (Greek notation marks). Like Hebrew cantillation marks, Greek neumes appear above or below the words in vocal music, rather than on separate staves (staff notation developed much later), verifying accounts that in Hellenic culture music was the handmaiden of poetry, and that its main function was to enhance the text.

The earliest known examples of solo songs date from the tenth century, but once again their notation is not fully understood. A famous thirteenth-century collection called *Carmina Burana* contains many solo songs, some of which are written in more modern notation. Several of the poems from this collection were used by Carl Orff in his "scenic cantata" *Carmina Burana* (1935–36).

Twelfth- and thirteenth-century songs—chansons de geste, lais, and rondeaux—were used primarily for storytelling purposes. Trouvères and troubadours, well-born French poets, sang their own texts to simple tunes and strummed accompaniments, or hired jongleurs, professional entertainers, to sing them. Notation for these songs is precise in matters of pitch but gives no indication of rhythm, for the metric stresses followed the words. Since French was the language of poetry in most of the civilized world at that time, the songs of the trouvères and troubadours were sung in England, Italy, and Spain as well as in France itself. In Germany minnesinger and meistersinger, amateur and craft musicians respectively, played roles comparable to those of the trouvères, troubadours, and jongleurs.

During the thirteenth and fourteenth centuries composed vocal music gradually became more complex as homophony, the single melodic line with simple accompaniment, yielded to polyphony, the combining of two or more independent horizontal voices. By the end of the fourteenth century it was not uncommon for three or four voices or groups of voices to sing simultaneously, each using a different melody and a different text. Sometimes the lines of verse were in different languages; often they were a mixture of secular and religious texts. Since the words were incomprehensible in these madrigals and motets, they became less important to listener and performer. Rules regulating the behavior of these polyphonic compositions were compiled, and composing became more of a specialty. On the other hand, folk songs retained their simplicity, their single-voiced melodies now often accompanied by parallel thirds and sixths.

Melodies were considered public domain, everyone borrowing freely from everyone else, so the same tune might be used for any number of texts, some suitable and some totally unrelated in sentiment. French musicians, of whom Guillaume de Machaut is the best known, continued to dominate the European scene, but a strong tradition of intricate madrigals in two or three parts was developing in Italy. Francesco Landino was the acknowledged master of this Italian school.

One widespread and popular form of the period was the canonic two-part song in which one voice "chases" the other by means of rapid imitative entries. Known in Italy as caccia, in Spain as caçà, and in France as chace, these lively numbers were encountered everywhere.

Two facts emerge from the wealth of material unearthed from the fourteenth century: music was an important omnipresent part of court life as well as common life, and almost all music was vocal.

The end of the Middle Ages brought refinement and elegance to vocal music. The classic form of the first half of the fifteenth century was the chanson in ballade style, one solo voice on top with a two-part instrumental accompaniment, but by midcentury the rondeau had become the favorite song form. Increasing interest in instrumental music is reflected in the practice of surrounding the rondeaux with instrumental preludes and postludes, but instruments were still very much subservient to the human voice. Most of the rhythms commonly found today—6/8, 9/8, 2/4, 3/4, and 4/4 —were already in evidence, and metric patterns were carefully noted. Concern with chord progressions and consonance marks the end of the century, as composers began thinking more along vertical and less along purely horizontal lines (that is to say more with the way the melodic strands combine with one another at any given point and less with the total freedom of each line).

The close bonds between words and music found in the storytelling songs of the troubadours, loosened beyond recognition by the complexities of fourteenth-century part songs, had not as yet been reestablished, but there was at least a rapport in sentiment between words and music in the song literature of the day. The most famous names of the period—and all were internationally known—are Guillaume Dufay, Jean d' Okeghem, Gilles Binchois, and John Dunstable.

The ability to print and publish large anthologies of music made hundreds of tunes available to English and European musicians during the sixteenth century. Any one melody might be found in a half-dozen guises—as the main line in a part song, for solo voice with instrumental accompaniment, as an instrumental solo, as an unaccompanied vocal line, in combination with other melodic lines by other composers, and so forth. Eminent composers such as Josquin Des Prés and Heinrich Isaac were even more internationally celebrated than their predecessors had been. There was a sophisticated audience for professionally composed songs and all forms flourished.

Although contradictory trends can be seen, there was some movement, exemplified by English composer William Byrd, to return to a closer relationship between words and music. This led to the development of the English lute song, of which the songs of John Dowland, printed first in 1597 and in several subsequent editions, are the epitome. In the songs of Dowland we find a genuine collaboration between vocalist and accompanist, making this skilled lutenist and composer a true precursor of Schubert and Schumann.

The first years of the seventeenth century saw the appearance of a group of Florentine musicians who wished to return to the simplicity of Greek music. These so-called monodists insisted on bringing music back to its position as servant to poetry, with all metrical, dynamic, and ornamental stresses dictated by the words. There were accompaniments to the single melodic lines, but they were composed of minimal chord sequences. While such brilliant composers as Jacopo Peri and Claudio Monteverdi espoused the aims of the monodists, they soon realized the limitations of their theories, and used the tenets as guides rather than dicta.

The influence of the Florentine monodists was widespread and intense, but short-lived. Their recitative-like dramatic monologues led directly to the solo cantata, a long form expressing varied emotions in contrasting recitative, arioso, and aria sections. The English lute song, while somewhat chastened by monodist theories, never really disappeared, and its influence may be heard in the songs of Purcell. In Germany the church cantata gradually replaced the solo song as the principal form of vocal expression; essential to its structure is the inclusion of a chorale which can be sung by the congregation. The French aristocracy, bemused by the splendor of the operatic presentations at the court of Louis XIV, where the composer Jean Baptiste Lully reigned supreme, turned its attention from the single solo song, but the tradition of folk song remained alive outside court circles.

From this rich tapestry of vocal music one pattern emerges: the constant pendulum swing from simplicity to complexity and back again. When the emphasis is on the words, clarity of texture is essential; when intricacy of contrapuntal musical devices is the overriding concern, the words become less important. In the greatest art songs of each period, the perfect balance is sought in the light of stylistic preferences of the day. Far from being resolved, the ambivalent attractions of simplicity and complexity continue to pull music first in one direction, then in the other, but in general the relatively simple homophonic accompaniment is best suited to the creation of great art songs.

Early Italian Songs

In the latter half of the seventeenth century several figures of great importance to the development of the art song appeared in Italy, composers whose names are somewhat familiar to modern audiences because recitalists frequently choose to open their programs with examples of this repertoire. Undoubtedly the best known of these early Italian songwriters is Alessandro Scarlatti (1660–1725), father of the even more renowned composer of over six hundred harpsichord sonatas, Domenico Scarlatti (1685–1757). Among others whose songs appear with some frequency are Marc' Antonio Cesti (1623–1669), Alessandro Stradella (1642–1682), Antonio Lotti (1667–1740), and Antonio Caldara (1670–1736).

Strictly speaking the output of these outstanding innovators does not come under the aegis of our study, for Alessandro Scarlatti and his contemporaries concentrated on opera to the virtual exclusion of the solo song; most of what we hear has been excerpted from their long dramatic works. Furthermore, during this period accompaniments for solo songs were seldom written out; performers were expected to improvise harmonic settings according to "figured bass" instructions, that is, numbers printed below the melodic line indicating crucial harmonies and chord positions. Sometimes even less information was given, nothing more than the "basso continuo," the moving bottom line, with no hint at harmonic intentions. The accompaniments we hear in recitals today are "realizations" or arrangements for modern keyboard, and are therefore not always authentic.

When an orchestral accompaniment was intended, the composer often left only vague suggestions as to the exact instrumentation. We know that great strides were made in orchestration at this time, trumpets and woodwinds having been introduced and the melodic role of the string section having been expanded as these instruments improved. Unfortunately little of the original flavor can be conveyed by the piano reductions now used in recital.

Even the melodic lines are suspect, for no matter how scrupulously they are copied from extant manuscripts, the seventeenth-century practice of free embellishments on the part of the singer places the editor in a dilemma: should he write in what scholars think are appropriate ornaments and flourishes, or should he leave the bare line and trust the musicianship of the modern-day interpreter?

Despite these problems many of the early Italian songs are too attractive to ignore. Most of the melodies, especially those in the minor mode, are tinged with gentle melancholy, but neither violent passion nor extreme pain is allowed to disturb the graceful serenity which is one of the salient characteristics of their style. Exaggerated contrasts, abrupt shifts of mood, harsh dissonances, and isolated high notes are usually avoided, but emotional depth is not absent.

Some of the songs are amusing, even comic, but again in a civilized, polished way. "Se Florindo è fedele" ("If Florindo

Is Faithful") by Alessandro Scarlatti, for example, has a bit of this levity, and is a very charming song indeed. The thought is simple—the young lady says that if Florindo is faithful, she'll fall in love with him; if not, she knows how to protect her heart from Cupid's bow. Voice and accompaniment playfully exchange little melodic scale-fragments throughout the piece, and the refrain, "m'innamorerò," "I shall fall in love" is set to a charming two-note figure which is almost like a slow trill. At the refrain the piano echoes the voice which is allowed complete rhythmic freedom.

The repeated use of one short sentence, "Se Florindo è fedele io m'innamorerò" for the opening and closing sections of this ABA song, marks it as closer in concept to an operatic aria than to a genuine art song.

A very beautiful example of a more serious song by this same composer is "O cessate di piagarmi" ("Oh, No Longer Seek to Pain Me"). The melodic line is made plaintive by the use of repeated notes followed by a half-step rise, and strict adherence to the minor scale. A line combining repeated notes and a gradual ascent creates considerable tension in contrast to the more pleading principal melody. Despite repetition of some lines of verse, the text is not distorted beyond the limits of art song usage.

In "Spesso vibra per suo gioco" ("Oft the Blindfold Boy"—Eros or Cupid) we find Scarlatti in a jovial mood again, this time expressing frivolity with a lively tarantella. Here too the words take second place to the music, and even the melody is subordinate to the rollicking rhythm.

Although many of these Italian songs are delightful in their own right, their chief importance is their influence on future song and opera composers. The facile grace and charm of their melodies made a great impression on Händel and Mozart; they are the necessary link between the antique and the modern art song.

Several of Scarlatti's songs can be heard on a London record (25726) featuring soprano Teresa Berganza. Other early Italian songs by Cesti, Stradella, and others have been recorded on the Pleiades label (S–103). The music for many of these songs has been published in collections by various firms, including a perfectly acceptable two-volume set (by G. Schirmer with English translations) called *Anthology of Italian Songs* (vols. 290 and 291).

Henry Purcell
(1659–1695)

Although Henry Purcell's dates place his life entirely within the seventeenth century, he might well be considered the first "modern" composer of art songs. Unlike his Italian counterparts (Alessandro Scarlatti was born one year after Purcell) he produced an enormous body of songs, writing almost a hundred secular solo songs, fifteen sacred songs for one voice, two sacred vocal duets, and some forty-three secular vocal duos. Added to this considerable output is an equally impressive number of incidental songs for the theater, plus six operas of which *Dido and Aeneas* is the best known.

The first song attributed with certainty to Purcell is found in an anthology published in 1676 called *Choice Ayres.* By that time the sixteen-year-old prodigy had a considerable reputation based on even earlier compositions, and he was soon reputed to be England's greatest composer. Indeed for generations he was England's only acknowledged musical genius.

Many of Purcell's songs are distinguished by his choice of exceptionally fine poetry as texts, works by John Dryden,

William Congreve, Tom Durfey, and Abraham Cowley. (His most famous song, however, "If Music Be the Food of Love," uses a poem by the obsure Hevengham, not the Shakespearean poem.) It is clear from his music that the words were of great importance to Purcell, for his syllabification is a model of clarity and sensitivity. Never does an ornament or melodic interval obscure the sound of a word; never does a metric stress contradict standard pronunciation.

Purcell's accompaniments usually consist of the standard "continuo," that is, a harpsichord with a viola da gamba (an early cello) to reinforce the weak bass notes of the keyboard instruments.

Among the representative examples of Purcell's art songs found on an album published by the Bach Guild (BGS–7057/1) are "If Music Be the Food of Love," "Not All My Torments," "The Fatal Hour Comes On Apace," "I Love and I Must," "The Blessed Virgin's Expostulation," and "Upon a Quiet Conscience." The first four named are solo secular songs; the last two are called sacred. There is no discernible difference in style between the sacred and secular songs; in fact the "Blessed Virgin's Expostulation" might easily be mistaken for a poignant love song.

From this small sampling of Purcell's songs the following characteristics emerge: extremely effective use of chromaticism to express despair* (the flatted top note on the word "sorrow" in "Not All My Torments"), florid ornamentation to emphasize key words ("large" and "hard" in "I Love and I Must"), dramatic use of rising and falling intervals and sequences of intervals (the rising sequence on "your eyes, your mien, your tongue" and the rising line on "so fierce" in "If Music Be the Food of Love"; the melodic fall on

---

*This psychologically insightful use of falling chromaticism is even more vividly displayed in Dido's final lament in *Dido and Aeneas*.

"grave" in "Not All My Torments"). The accompaniments show little true independence, although in "I Love and I Must" the harpsichord introduces the melody at each entry.

Perhaps the most beautiful of the six songs here discussed is the sacred duo, "Upon a Quiet Conscience—Close Thine Eyes." The soprano begins the song alone, and for the first four lines the baritone follows the soprano in canonic imitation. For this section, and again for the last line of verse, the two voices weave a gorgeous two-part texture, the accompaniment providing a third strand. In lines 5 through 9 the two voices sing in serene harmony, a beautiful contrast to the polyphonic texture of the opening section. At the words "music and mirth" the song quickens in tempo, describing musically the livelier feeling implied by the words. The end is once again beatific and serene. A more beautiful blending of words and music is hard to imagine.

Georg Friedrich Händel
(1685–1759)

and Johann Sebastian Bach
(1685–1750)

Musical wags maintain that the best Spanish music was written by Frenchmen and that the greatest English composer was a German. While "best" and "greatest" are treacherous words in the subjective world of the arts, few would deny that Georg Friedrich Händel, born and educated in Germany and strongly influenced by his years in Italy (1706–10), was for generations England's best-known and best-loved composer.

Händel's first visit to England took place in 1710, by which time he had already composed five operas, two oratorios, one secular choral work, four of the twenty Italian chamber duets, three German Songs, seven French Songs, six Trio Sonatas for two oboes and continuo, a Sonata for viola da gamba and continuo, and assorted religious vocal music. Nevertheless, naturalized as an Englishman, enjoying the personal patronage of three successive English rulers (Queen Anne, George I, and George II), and basing most of his famous oratorios, including *Esther, Israel in Egypt, Samson, Judas Maccabaeus,* and the ubiquitous *Messiah,* on English texts, Händel does indeed deserve to be called an Englishman.

Like his illustrious contemporary, Johann Sebastian Bach, Händel was enormously prolific. Unlike Bach, for whom vocal musical expression was almost exclusively devotional, Händel wrote dozens of secular operas, choral works, cantatas, and vocal chamber pieces. Even his biblical oratorios were conceived as celebrations and entertainments rather than as part of any religious ritual.

Since Bach and Händel represent the culmination of the Baroque period, they have many characteristics in common. Basic to their style is fugal texture, the interweaving of quasi-independent melodic lines, wedded to a solid harmonic substructure. Both composers excelled in building imposing architectonic edifices such as Bach's *Art of Fugue, Musical Offering,* and B Minor Mass, or Händel's great oratorios. These massive works, with their interlocking key relationships, display an awesome unity of concept and expression.

Neither Bach nor Händel is really known for his individual secular songs—Bach seems to have written only a few slender examples, putting words to five of the little teaching pieces he composed for his bride Anna Magdalena—but Händel's output in the idiom of vocal chamber-music is rich, varied, and worthy of study. We have chosen for discussion four pieces of vocal chamber-music by Händel: the Italian Duets Nos. 2 and 20, the Italian Trio No. 1, and the second of the Nine German Songs of 1729. The Duet No. 2 and the Trio No. 1 are early works (ca. 1708) and the Duet No. 20 is quite late (1745). The German Song may be found on Musical Heritage Society record MHS 722S, the others on Musical Heritage Society record MHS 1453.

Händel composed a total of twenty Italian chamber duets and two Italian trios. Each of these works lasts from five to ten minutes and is in at least two contrasting sections. Only the first few were composed while Händel was in Italy, but all of them, even those written much later, show Italian-ate grace and fluidity. They differ from their counterparts by Italian composers in that they are quite homogeneous in texture, showing no rigorous alternation between solo and tutti passages. Although many have occasional recitative-like (homophonic, declamatory) passages, they are basically contrapuntal, the continuo part adding a third or fourth horizontally conceived line to the two or three vocal parts.

Händel often used the later Duets as sketches for his large choral works. In Duet No. 15 (1741) we hear music far more familiar to us as "His Yoke Is Easy" and "He Shall Purify" from *Messiah* (1742); in Duet No. 16 (1741) we find "For Unto Us a Child Is Born" and "All We Like Sheep," which are also in *Messiah*. Of course it was far from uncommon for composers of the period to use the same material in several works—Bach did it frequently.

Duet No. 2, "Giu nei tartarei regni," uses a text by the Italian poet Ortensio Mauro. Its two protagonists, a soprano and a baritone, accuse each other of loving too little, while each claims to love too much. The words burn with passion:

> Down in the Tartarean realm we shall go my lady.
> I shall be damned for having loved too much (He)
> You will be damned for having loved too little (She)
> Burning with ardour I shall be thrown into the coldest place
> But, as the utmost cold
> Is in your heart, and the utmost ardour is in mine,
> We shall abide together in eternity.
> I shall be in your heart
> And you in mine, hell for both.

As one might expect given this ardent text, the music of the opening is intensely dramatic. The baritone enters first, his deep voice emphasizing the crucial falling interval of the melodic line. The soprano follows in imitation and the two sing in two-part polyphony, the third part supplied by the continuo.* At "Burning with ardour" the music quickens in tempo and the mood seems to brighten. "But, as the utmost cold" is sung in harmony—like a recitative—interrupting the fugal texture, but from "Is in your heart" to the end we return to the contrapuntal style. The entire piece is operatic in effect.

The last of the Italian Duets, "Ah! nelle sorti umane," was composed some thirty-three years after "Giu nei tartarei regni," but the style is not discernibly different. The poignant andante opening shows more maturity, perhaps, and there is an effective instrumental interlude before the second section, but the salient features—fugal texture combined

---

*While the continuo requires two players, harpsichord and viola da gamba, it is considered to be only one "voice" or part. This is because the viola da gamba merely reinforces the harpsichord, contributing no new thematic material.

with beautiful chordal cadences, dramatic contrast between sections, evocative rapport between words and music—remain. The author of this text is unknown:

> Ah! In human destinies
> The greatest happiness
> Is not without anguish!
>
> But vain hopes
> Lure the mind into thinking
> That pain and pleasure go hand in hand.

The music for the first three lines (in all these works each line of verse is repeated many times) is melancholy, the two soprano voices expressing sorrow appropriate to the words. After a brief instrumental interlude in which the music of this section is reworked, the mood becomes much livelier. At the word "pain" there is a sudden shift to the minor mode, and it is not until the final chord that we hear a return to the major. Major endings to compositions in the minor mode were common in the Baroque era and always make an interesting effect.

For Trio No. 1 (1708), "Se tu non lasci amore," we again have a text by Mauro:

> If you do not leave me, my love,
> My heart, you wi'l repent, I know it.
>
> But whom am I speaking to, oh, God!
>
> When I have no more heart
> Or when the heart I have is no longer mine.

Since there are three singers and the continuo we now have four-part polyphony. The piece opens with three successive entries of the thematic material, the two sopranos first and then the baritone. All the usual contrapuntal devices are present—imitative entries, sequences (patterns of notes repeated on several pitch levels), inversions, and so forth. There is an instrumental interlude between lines 1 and 2 and a nonfugal recitative for "But whom am I speaking to, oh, God!" The last two lines are sung to livelier music, although the words are no more cheerful than they were in the beginning.

Perhaps the most beautiful of the works selected for discussion here is "Das Zitternde Glänzen der spielenden Wellen," a trio for soprano, violin, and continuo, the second of the nine German Songs composed in 1729. The German poet Barthold Heinrich Brockes supplied the texts for all nine pieces.

> The shimmering sparkle of frolicsome waves
> Silvers the shore, heaps pearls of foam on its rim.
>
> The rustling streams, the bubbling springs
> Make fruitful the land, and black and moist.
>
> In countless wondrous ways, they make it known—
> The goodness of God who created us all.

Händel opens the piece with a gorgeous instrumental section in which the violin introduces the main melodic line. This melody is free-flowing and extremely expressive. The violin becomes silent as the soprano enters in imitation of the original line. When the soprano moves to a more static contrapuntal line, the violin reenters with the more flowery melody. The two then exchange material for the remainder of the section (the first two lines of verse).

At "The rustling streams" new material is introduced for the contrasting section. The violin has some particularly virtuosic figurations and there is more ornamentation in general. The da capo (the repeat of the A section in this ABA form) is heralded by the reiteration of the instrumental prelude, after which the entire first section is heard again. A lovely obbligato passage in which soprano and violin sing in thirds brings the work to an end.

Considering the enduring popularity of Händel's oratorios—no Christmas is official without multitudinous performances of *Messiah*—it is strange that these vocal chamber-works should be so little known. Perhaps as vocal chamber-music becomes a more popular art form, this area of Händel's creative genius will be more appreciated.

Franz Joseph Haydn
(1732–1809)

Franz Joseph Haydn's instrumental output is so voluminous that aside from his great choral works, of which *Creation* is probably the most often heard, his considerable contribution to the vocal repertoire tends to be overlooked. Nevertheless he composed 18 operas, 14 Masses, 11 choral works with orchestra, about 40 cantatas, some 50 songs for solo voice with piano accompaniment, and almost 500 settings for Scottish, Irish, and Welsh folk tunes. When we remember that his instrumental works include 104 symphonies, 83 string quartets, 31 trios for piano, violin, and cello, 52 piano sonatas, 66 string trios, 125 trios including the baryton (a kind of tuba played by his patron, Prince Nicolaus Esterházy), 37 concerti, and dozens of assorted duos and divertimenti, we can see why some of his compositions receive little attention, but the relative obscurity of the songs is undeserved, for many of them are very lovely and a few are of the first order.

Haydn was the earliest of the great triumvirate of composers of the Classic era. With Mozart (1756–1791) and Beethoven (1770–1827) he created and brought to an unequaled peak the musical forms known as symphony, concerto, string quartet, and sonata. Many of the characteristics of the instrumental writing of this period are found in contemporary songs; the only tenet of classicism we cannot extrapolate from the songs is the classicists' concern for structure, which is exemplified by the pervasive use of sonata form.

The chief difference between the songs of Purcell and Händel on the one hand, and those of all the composers who follow on the other, a difference which immediately strikes the ear of even the most unsophisticated listener, is the change from the fugal texture of the earlier compositions to the homophonic texture of those which came later. This is true even of vocal chamber-music, where several voices may sing at once. In Baroque music each voice is given a quasi-independent melodic line—"quasi" because there are necessary accommodations for the chordal substructure. In music of the Classic era there is one independent melodic line, usually on top, plus a harmonic accompaniment. Hence if two voices sing at once, their melodic lines are regulated by predominantly harmonic considerations; a quartet of singers will sing in four-part harmony rather than in four-part polyphony. Again, the difference is much easier to hear than to describe.

This does not mean that there are no countermelodies in a post-Baroque song, nor does it mean that no symphony or sonata contains fugal passages (many in fact do). It simply indicates that composers' preferences had turned once again to a simpler homophonic sound.

To many this new texture, with its clear-cut distinction between melody and accompaniment, marks the true beginning of the modern art song. Since Händel lived until 1759 and Haydn was born in 1732, there is obviously much overlap. Thus one finds homophonic arias in many of Händel's operas and oratorios. Other composers, including the sons of

Johann Sebastian Bach, also span the two periods, and the great Bach himself was aware at the end of his life (he died in 1750) of being "old-fashioned" in his preference for polyphony.

The "new" homophonic sound did not spring full-blown from any one composer's head. It developed from a conscious desire to abandon the complexities of polyphonic composition—a position similar to that of the seventeenth-century Florentine monodists—coupled with a new emphasis on key relationships and chord progressions. In general classicism implies preoccupation with formal structure, nobility of concept, restraint in emotional display, and universality of appeal. Haydn's works, leavened by the spontaneity and variety of their melodic invention, are exemplary manifestations of the classic spirit.

We have chosen four of Haydn's better-known songs for discussion: "Das Leben ist ein Traum," published in 1784 as one of the Twelve Songs with Clavier; "She Never Told Her Love" and "My Mother Bids Me Bind My Hair" from the English canzonets of 1794 and 1795; and "The Spirit's Song," published separately after the canzonets but often included as one of them.* The first two may be heard on an Allegro record (A 13); the others are part of Marian Anderson's farewell recital recorded by RCA Victor in 1964 (RCA LSC–2781).

The first characteristic of these songs to strike the listener is the expressive role of the piano accompaniment. Each one has a piano introduction in which the mood of the entire piece is set; when the words require a change of mood it is often a piano interlude that first expresses the emotional

---

*Interestingly enough, three of the four are set by Haydn in the original English although he was not really that familiar with the language.

shift. Several harmonic devices recur—a false cadence before the final ending, a minor chord under a melodic note previously supported by a major tonality, a diminished chord for dramatic emphasis, a suspension to create tension. All these effects may be found in abundance in Haydn's instrumental compositions.

"Das Leben ist ein Traum" ("Life Is a Dream") is a serious, philosophical poem for which Haydn provides an appropriately pensive, dignified setting. Its major tonality (E flat major in the original) prevents a feeling of tragedy or despair, though the text touches on the heartbreak of love. The poem's two stanzas are set strophically; in each verse a question, "Was ist, was *ist* das Leben?" ("What is life?") is treated dramatically, but the answer, "Life is a dream," restores calm. The melodic line is simple with very little ornamentation as befits the serious nature of the text, but its freeflowing phrases are filled with grace and beauty.

"She Never Told Her Love" is taken from act II, scene IV of Shakespeare's *Twelfth Night*, in which Viola, disguised as a young man, tries to conceal and yet reveal her love for the Duke. Haydn uses only part of Viola's speech:

> She never told her love,
> But let concealment, like a worm i' the bud,
> Feed on her damask cheek:
> . . . .
> She sat like Patience on a monument,
> Smiling at grief.

The song is through-composed. Although it seems very brief for its content, it manages to make its point musically. There is a rather long piano introduction after which the voice enters plaintively but in the major mode (A flat major in the original). On the middle syllable of the word "concealment" there is a flatted melodic note (not found in all editions) which gives a sinister, foreboding cast to the word. If you don't know the play you might really wonder just what she's hiding! The words "sat" and "patience" are supported by lugubrious minor chords, and the first "grief"—"Smiling at grief" is repeated—has a menacing false-cadence diminished chord.

Some critics have found the dramatically emotive style of this song inappropriate to Viola's words in this entertainment by Shakespeare for the Feast of Epiphany (the play was first presented on the twelfth night of Christmas). Since the song was not intended for inclusion in the play, the criticism seems unwarranted—the music certainly suits the words when taken at face value.

"My Mother Bids Me Bind My Hair," officially titled "A Pastoral Song," is probably Haydn's best-known song. It is in ABAB form, the contrasting music for stanzas 1 and 2 repeated exactly for stanzas 3 and 4. Once again we are in the major mode—relatively few of Haydn's songs are in the minor—with occasional appropriate excursions into the minor. The poem is by a Mrs. John Hunter:

> My mother bids me bind my hair,
> With bands of rosy hue;
> Tie up my sleeves with ribands rare,
> And lace my bodice blue.
>
> For why, she cries, sit still and weep
> While others dance and play?
> Alas I scarce can go, or creep,
> While Lubin is away.
>
> 'Tis sad to think the days are gone
> When those we love are near;
> I sit upon this mossy stone
> And sigh when none can hear.
>
> And while I spin my flaxen thread
> And sing my simple lay,

The village seems asleep or dead
Now Lubin is away.

The tune begins with a lighthearted A major (tonic) triad
which establishes the simple, pastoral mood. The carefree
tone of the music continues through the first stanza. A piano
interlude between stanzas 1 and 2 introduces a poignant minor sound, and even though we shift back to major when the
voice reenters, the innocent gaiety is gone.

When Haydn set "The Spirit's Song" to music, he
thought he was once again dealing with a text by Shakespeare. Perhaps the words made him think of the ghost of
Hamlet's father, for the foreboding octaves in the lower registers of the piano with which the song begins might well be
walking music for that "martial stalk" on the ramparts of
Elsinore. The words, by an unknown poet, give us no real
clue as to the identity of the spirit:

Hark! what I tell to thee
Nor sorrow o'er the tomb
My spirit wanders free
And waits till thine shall come.

All pensive and alone,
I see thee sit and weep,
Thy heart upon the stone,
Where my cold ashes sleep.

I watch thy speaking eyes
And mark each falling tear,
I catch thy passing sighs,
Ere they are lost in air.

The long piano introduction features a startling chord at the
end of the opening melodic octaves. This idea is repeated,
and at the second frightening chord the voice enters with the

single word "Hark." On the line "My spirit wanders free," piano and voice rise chromatically in unison, adding to the already considerable dramatic tension.

The piano interlude before "All pensive and alone" is replete with repeated notes, which give a sense of urgency to the whole middle section. Increasing the tempo for this B section lessens its impact and should be avoided (no such più mosso is indicated, but some performers seem to feel it).

After "Ere they are lost in air" we have a repeat of the original piano introduction, which leads to a recapitulation of the opening four-line stanza. This time at the line "My spirit wanders free," Haydn gives us a descending chromatic line, the mirror image of the ascending chromatic passage in the first section. A false cadence at "till thine shall come" necessitates a repeat of the final line to bring the song to a proper close. Thus the second A of this essentially ABA song differs slightly—and most effectively—from the first.

Wolfgang Amadeus Mozart
(1756–1791)

With the songs of Wolfgang Amadeus Mozart, we finally arrive at repertoire commonly included in present-day art song recitals. Nevertheless, of his thirty-six songs for solo voice and piano accompaniment only a half-dozen or so are really familiar to song recital audiences. The reason for this is simple—with one or two exceptions only these few represent Mozart at his best, for included in the three dozen are many slight pieces, generally strophic in structure, whose minimal piano accompaniments do little but reinforce the singer's melodic line. Even these lesser efforts have the charm and grace so characteristic of Mozart, and we shall discuss two of them—"Die kleine Spinnerin" and "Sehnsucht nach dem Frühling." Of the more important songs we shall discuss the following: "Das Veilchen," "Abendempfindung," "Als Luise die Briefe ihres ungetreuen Liebhabers verbrannte," "An Chloë," and "Der Zauberer." All may be heard on Vanguard record VRS 481; "Das Veilchen" and "Abendempfindung" are also included on a Seraphim record devoted to German art songs (SIC–6072).

Since the piano parts and vocal lines of these songs are relatively simple, anyone with a few years of piano lessons in his past might enjoy playing and singing them. The Peters Edition (vol. 9536) edited by Max Friedlaender is clear and contains all the best songs, but unfortunately does not supply English translations of the texts; the Kalmus edition (vol. 6322) is a little harder to read but has the advantage of English translations.

In 1781 Haydn and Mozart met for the first time. Each fully appreciated the other's genius; both knew they had no equals. The exchange of ideas between the twenty-five-year-old Mozart and the master almost twice his age was fruitful for both; after that date each reached new peaks of greatness. All the Haydn songs discussed in the preceding chapter were written after 1781—in fact the last three were composed after Mozart's tragically premature death in 1791 (Haydn lived until 1809). These late Haydn songs show Mozart's influence in their enriched harmonic palette and almost operatic sense of drama; Mozart clearly benefited from Haydn's sense of structure, especially in the through-composed songs.

"Die kleine Spinnerin" (1787) and "Sehnsucht nach dem Frühling" (1791) might easily be mistaken for songs of Mozart's youth, for both are naive, folklike settings of innocent little poems. The first, "The Little Spinner," is a dialogue in which a young lad named Fritz tries to tempt a maiden away from her spinning. He wants her to come and play, but she says that play brings trouble, for men seduce young girls only to leave them, so she'll keep out of trouble by continuing to spin. The mood is coquettish and flirtatious. The second, "Yearning for Spring," calls for sweet May to come and make the violet bloom. In successive verses it describes the pleasures of the other seasons, but extols the charms of May above all, for May brings violets, nightingales, and cuckoos.

"The Little Spinner" has three verses, the first by an unknown poet, the second and third by von Daniel Jager; "Yearning for Spring" has five, all by Christian Adolf Overbeck. In both songs the vocal parts and accompaniments are repeated note for note for all stanzas. The sole concession to the words comes at the end of the fifth stanza of "Yearning for Spring," when the pianist, according to a tradition *not* indicated in the score, changes the phrasing of the last measure to imitate the sound of the cuckoo. This strophic structure was by far the most popular song form in the eighteenth century, and it has never in fact been totally abandoned.

The settings for "Yearning for Spring" and "The Little Spinner" are both simple enough to be folk tunes. The former begins with a melody derived from the tonic triad, the first, third, and fifth notes of the main scale of the piece (F major for high voice in this song). This naive little phrase is heard at the beginning of three of the four lines of each stanza—only the third line, "Wie möcht' ich doch so gerne ein Veilchen wieder sehn" in the first stanza, begins with different material. The accompaniment follows the vocalist's line with the right hand, and supports the melody with broken tonic and dominant* chords in the left. There is a charming

---

*A dominant chord consists of a triad whose lowest note is the fifth note in the main scale. Often the seventh tone is added to this new 1/3/5 making a dominant-seventh chord (V-7). In the key of F this dominant-seventh chord would be composed of C/E/G/ and B flat.

little postlude after each stanza in which the piano has bird-like trills.

The plan for "The Little Spinner" is just as uncompli-cated. Again the main melody is derived from the tonic triad (all bugle calls and most nursery tunes are variations of this basic combination of notes). Since the young maiden is bus-ily spinning, the music is designed to convey the feeling of perpetual motion, with no held notes or rests. No attempt is made however to imitate the whirring of a spinning wheel as Schubert was to do so magnificently a scant twenty-seven years later in "Gretchen am Spinnrade."

"Der Zauberer" is also strophic in structure, but its melody and harmonic background are much more sophisti-cated than the two songs discussed above. The title may be translated as "The Magician" or "Enchanter"; its poem, by C. F. Weisse, tells of a young girl who was swept off her feet by a man so enchanting she thinks he must have been a sorcerer. After all, she says, he made her turn red, he made her turn white; she must have been in a trance, for she couldn't hear his words; she followed him into the woods blindly—it's a good thing her mother came along or who knows what might have happened!

Mozart's setting well conveys the tension in the little story. The piano has a brief but tempestuous introductory measure—really a flourish to set the stage. The voice enters with the notes of the tonic triad, but since we are in the minor mode (G minor for high voice) even this much-used sequence seems less naive. Agitated chords in the accompaniment con-vey the girl's excitement and anxiety, as does the rising chro-matic line under "ich seufzte, zitterte, und schien mich doch zu freùn" ("I sighed and trembled yet seemed to be filled with joy"). A final cascade of notes in the piano part brings each verse to an animated and virtuosic close. Of course we are not meant to be too worried by this youthful adventure, and the music has just the right flavor of titillating suspense.

Of the many other strictly strophic Mozart songs, "Die Alte" is probably the most interesting, because of its minor key and the strong false cadence near the end. "Trennungslied," a beautiful and unique variation of the genre, has four verses in a strophic setting, a fifth and sixth for which Mozart composed fresh material, and a recapitulation of the original music for the final (seventh) stanza. This gives it a combination ABA-strophic form.

Another of Mozart's simpler songs worthy of mention is "An Chloë," whose music reminds one of the delightful soubrette arias found in his operas. One of its most interesting features is the use of ornamental variations in the melody.

The three songs discussed below are Mozart's most important contributions to the repertoire. "Das Veilchen" ("The Violet") is probably the most highly regarded of all Mozart's songs, as much because of its superior text by Goethe as for its beautiful music. The poem is a poignant one:

> Ein Veilchen auf der Wiese stand / gebückt in sich und unbekannt:
> es war ein herzig's Veilchen! / Da kam ein' junge Schäferin / mit leichtem Schritt und munterm Sinn, / daher, daher, / die Wiese her und sang.
>
> "Ach!" denkt das Veilchen, wär' ich nur / die schönste Blume der Natur, / "ach!" nur ein kleines Veilchen,
> bis mich das Liebchen abgepflückt / und an dem Busen matt gedrückt, / "ach nur, ach nur / ein Viertelstündchen lang!"
>
> Ach, aber ach! das Mädchen kam / und nicht in Acht das Veilchen nahm, / ertrat das arme Veilchen.
> Es sank und starb und freut' sich noch: / "und sterb' ich denn, so sterb' ich doch / durch sie, durch sie, zu ihren Füssen doch!"
> Das arme Veilchen! / Es war ein herzig's Veilchen!
>
> A violet grew in meadow green
> Content to blossom all unseen,

Oh! 'twas a dainty violet!
A shepherdess once came that way;
So light her step, her laugh so gay;
And as she went she sang merrily
"Ah!" said the violet, "if only I were the fairest flower in all of nature,
If only for a moment, Until my love could gather me
And bury me in her bosom, I should be content to die on her breast."
Alas! alas! The maid came and did not see the violet in the grass, but crushed the poor violet!
It bowed its head and gently died. "Oh! 'tis for her sweet sake," it cried. "For her, for her, as at her feet I lie!"
Ah! hapless violet! it was a dainty violet!

The piano begins the song alone with a full statement of the main melodic line. This phrase is unusual in that it consists of seven rather than the customary eight bars. (Most pre-twentieth-century music is in phrases that are multiples of four measures.) This one-measure abbreviation has the effect of truncating the phrase, making its end somewhat abrupt. Since the song closes with the last three measures of this introductory passage, the ending also seems somewhat abrupt, and in fact the song has been criticized for its precipitous close.

The voice enters with an exact repeat of the introductory melody. As the song continues, the accompaniment interprets the words, first by staccato notes to imitate the shepherdess's "dainty steps" (under the words "leichtem Schritt und munterm Sinn," "light steps and carefree spirit") and then in an interlude which is obviously the maiden's song (after the words "die Wiese her und sang," "through the meadow singing"). The voice reenters wistfully and the music shifts to the major mode as the violet thinks of the bliss that would be his if he were to be picked by the maiden.

When he sings "Ach nur, ach nur ein Viertel-stundchen lang," "Oh, only for a quarter of an hour", the accompaniment has a diminished and then a minor chord, lamenting the brevity of life and love. Supported by rhythmically agitated chords, the melody rises feverishly as the words tell us that the maiden has inadvertently crushed the violet. A fermata (a sign indicating that the performer should extend the time value) over a rest brings a long pause, after which the melody descends in pathetic two-note sighing phrases. Again we shift to the major mode as the violet bravely, heroically, says he doesn't mind, because at least he dies for the beautiful maiden. The last phrase, taken from the end of the opening statement, is the storyteller's brief comment on the drama he has just related.

This is a beautiful example of a through-composed song. Each phrase of the music is inspired by an individual line of verse. There are no real repeats but the recall of the early material for use as the final phrase connects the beginning to the end. Since the words and music are so expressively united, we need no preconceived musical structure to provide symmetry.

"Abendempfindung" ("Evening Song"), is another wonderful through-composed song. Its poem, by an unknown poet, is philosophical and at times melancholy, but with no feeling of tragedy or despair. It speaks of the brevity of life which is like a dream of rare delight. When life has ended, let a tear fall on the grave for friendship's sake. A friend's tear is like a jewel on a diadem, the fairest of all jewels.

Since the opening lines describe a serene, moonlit evening, Mozart begins his setting with a gently flowing accompanying figure based on the major tonic triad. The vocal line is calm, with many sustained notes. The words "so entflieh'n des Lebens schönste Stunden" ("so life's happiest moments fly away") are crucial to the poem's meaning, so Mozart allows them to stand out in bold relief by breaking off the flowing accompaniment and substituting stark chords. This alternation of accompanying figures continues through the song. At "des Freundes Träne" ("friends' tears") Mozart introduces the minor mode which predominates for the next several lines. The thought of his friends' tears brings comfort to the poet and before the words "Weih mir ein Träne" ("Consecrate one tear to me") we return to the serene mood and major modality of the opening section. The melodic line is not a recapitulation of the original, however, because the words are now more agitated and therefore require a different setting.

Interesting unifying devices may be noted in the music. For example the descending melodic line for the words "Aus ist unser Spiel!" is repeated in the piano part in the next measure; these same four notes reappear in the melody with the top note flatted four bars later. Most telling is the way the flowing, broken-chord figure restores the characteristic texture of the accompaniment after each dramatic break. The subtlety with which the music for the words "mir weht, wie West-wind leise, eine stille Ahnung zu" ("the silent presentment comes over me gently as the west wind") expresses the hushed expectancy conveyed by the text is just one example of the splendid unity of expression found in this song.

The longest title on record for a short song may very well be "Als Luise die Briefe ihres ungetreuen Liebhabers verbrannte"* ("When Louise destroyed the letters of her false lover"). This brief song, with its impassioned text by Gabriele von Baumberg, seethes with drama. Its single-measure piano prelude-postlude crackles with anger and foreboding; its wide opening melodic interval heralds Louise's passionate outburst. We are in the minor mode until after the

---

*The Kalmus edition uses the shorter title "Unglückliche Liebe" ("Love's Fatal Flame").

word "Melancholie," but even with the insertion of a section in the relative major (the major key with the same sharps or flats) we feel no soothing effect—the storm still rages in Louise's bosom. For the words "Ihr brennet nun, und bald, ihr Lieben, ist keine Spur von euch mehr hier" ("You are burning now, and soon, dear friends, there will be left no trace of you"), Mozart gives us an agitated rising melodic line and a breathless, chromatic accompaniment, both mounting in dynamic level to a tremendous climax. The piano continues with a heartbreaking descending line which features powerfully dissonant sounds created by an F sharp in the right hand against a G natural in the left and, after the voice reenters, a B natural on top against a C natural on bottom. This is another remarkably apt union of music and words, for at this point Louise admits that, even though her lover is untrue, her heart still cherishes the fatal flame of fierce desire—the deathless flame of fierce desire—for him.

Hearing these gems by Mozart, one regrets that this master did not choose to devote more serious attention to the art song, for it is clear that in the area of vocal music, opera presented a more interesting challenge to him. In truth it is not until Schubert that we find a major composer for whom art song was a vital, indispensable form of musical expression.

Ludwig van Beethoven
(1770–1827)

Although Ludwig van Beethoven's contribution to the development of the art song is modest, his position as one of the great geniuses of the world of music demands that we include an exploration of his songs in our study. His output in the vocal field is highly variable, including one opera, *Fidelio,* which has always elicited a mixture of criticism and praise from connoisseurs; three great choral works, the Mass in D major known as *Missa Solemnis,* the choral movement of the Ninth Symphony, and the *Choral Fantasy;* many little-known Masses and cantatas for chorus and orchestra; and almost one hundred solo songs with piano accompaniment.

Preoccupation with vocal music is manifested throughout Beethoven's life. In 1793 he began to study with the Italian opera composer Antonio Salieri (1750–1825), who was particularly helpful to Beethoven in matters of prosody, the musical syllabification of words. The arialike song "Adelaide" (Opus 46), which will be discussed below, comes from this period (1795) and shows Salieri's influence. The years 1803–5 were replete with vocal music, beginning with Beethoven's dashing off dozens of folk-song settings on commission, proceeding with six very lovely religious songs to texts by Christian Fürchtegott Gellert of which we shall discuss the fourth, "Die Ehre Gottes aus der Natur" (Opus 48 No. 4) and culminating in the completion of *Fidelio.*

In search of a libretto for a second opera—a project never to reach fruition—Beethoven turned his attention to the Faust legend as told by the great German poet Goethe. From this came the comic song "Der Floh" ("The Flea"), (Opus 75 No. 3, 1809) which Moussorgsky was to set to music exactly seventy years later (see page 164).

One of the most beautiful of Beethoven's songs, "An die Hoffnung" (Opus 94), was composed at the beginning of one of the composer's least productive periods, 1815–20, a time when Beethoven was outwardly preoccupied with family feuds and legal battles over custody of his nephew Karl and inwardly beginning his heroic struggles with the *Missa Solemnis* and the Ninth Symphony.* During this ostensibly

---

*Even these problems pale beside the all-consuming battle raging in his soul—the coming to grips with his growing deafness.

fallow time Beethoven wrote a major song-cycle, *An die ferne Geliebte* (Opus 98) based on six romantic poems by Jeitteles. We shall consider the first segment of the cycle. Last on our list is Beethoven's penultimate song, "Der Kuss" (Opus 128), written in 1822.

From the first example to the last we shall have spanned twenty-seven years, the years roughly approximating Beethoven's first and second creative periods. The first period is characterized by evidence of strong influences of other composers—in instrumental music of Haydn and Mozart, in vocal music of Italian opera as well. The second period, usually said to have begun with the Third Symphony, the *Eroica* (1803), shows the mature, powerful, earthshaking titan. After the *Missa Solemnis* and Ninth Symphony, both of which appeared in 1823 after four to five years of agonizing work, Beethoven became more introspective, less bombastic, more cerebral. He turned from the huge sound of chorus and orchestra, from the virtuosic keyboard solo, and from song to the austere demands of the string quartet.

While it is quite possible to taste the full range of Beethoven's creativity by studying his thirty-two piano sonatas, the last five of which foreshadow the thinking and style of the string quartets of the last period, one cannot glean the measure of the man from just the songs. Many of the songs are monotonously and endlessly strophic, few have the dramatic intensity of his instrumental works, and none has the intellectual strength of the late quartets. Nevertheless the good songs are very good indeed and far too seldom encountered. Kalmus has published sixty-six of the songs in one volume; Schirmer's has a separate edition of the cycle *An die ferne Geliebte.* Of the songs described below, "Der Floh" may be found on a Seraphim disc (S 60180) devoted to Beethoven's comic songs, and in a three-record album called *The Seraphim Guide to German Lieder* which also includes "Die Ehre Gottes aus der Natur"; *An die ferne Geliebte*, "Der Kuss," and "Adelaide" are included on the Westminster record XWN 18706.

"Adelaide" is a long rambling song in which the poet, Friedrich von Matthisson, rhapsodically compares his love to all the beauties of nature. He sees her face in the lake, on the snowy mountains. She will be the one flower to bloom on his grave. At the end of each verse we have a refrain composed of the five syllables of her name, A-de-la-i-de, sung like a caress. The song strongly resembles an Italian aria in its alternation of andante (slow) and allegro (fast) sections and in its diffuse nature. There are onomatopoeic touches, especially the trills used to suggest the song of the nightingale.

Although Beethoven was not an orthodox churchgoer, he was a deeply religious person who found God in the wonders of creation. In "Die Ehre Gottes aus der Natur," literally translated as "Praise of God from Nature" but known in England as "Creation's Hymn," Beethoven found the perfect text through which to express his feelings:

> The heavens praise the glory of the Everlasting,
> and the sound carries forth His name.
> The earth's circle praises him and the seas;
> hear, Oh, man, their divine word!
> Who holds aloft the numberless stars of heaven?
> Who leads the sun from under its tent?
> The sun comes shining and smiling from afar
> and goes its way like a hero.

The music is strong, virile, heroic. Its weighty accompanying chords make it sound almost angry at times, but the sudden dynamic drops to piano at "hear, Oh, man," and "Who holds aloft" bring a feeling of tender reverence. The last line, "und läuft den Weg, gleich als ein Held," is sung twice, first to an exhilarating rising line of heroic force and then to an equally affirmative final cadence.

Beethoven is well-known for his boisterous, earthy sense

of humor which sometimes arouses chuckles even in his instrumental music. One need look no further than the third and fourth movements of his Opus 1 No. 1, a trio for piano, violin, and cello, for an example. It is therefore no surprise that comic texts appealed to him—"Der Floh" is one of several such songs. The poem, in three eight-lines stanzas, tells of a "Once-upon-a-time" king who loved a big, fat flea as though he were his own son. He had his tailor outfit the flea in velvets and silks, made him a minister, made his relatives courtiers, and forbade anyone at court—even the queen—to pick the fleas off or scratch them away. At the very end of the song—for a repeat of the last two lines—a chorus of ordinary citizens enters to sing gleefully that they can crush the fleas whenever they like! (Beethoven was outspoken in his democratic feelings so the thought of the common man being better off than the courtiers must have delighted him!)

Beethoven's setting is most amusing. High grace notes and trills depict the flea; pompous bass-note octaves ridicule officious courtiers; the minor key lends an air of inflated importance and mock seriousness to the whole proceeding. The three stanzas are treated strophically, each ending on a questioning rising interval, but the choral recapitulation of the last two lines brings the song to a rousing beer-hall close.

Beethoven composed two settings for Tiedge's poem "An die Hoffnung." The first, Opus 32, was written about ten years earlier than the second, which we here consider.

Tiedge's words clearly aroused great tenderness in Beethoven, for this song is one of his most touching. The poem is in three stanzas and we quote the first:

Die du so gern in heil' gen Nächten feierst,
und sanft und weich den Gram verschleierst,
der eine zarte Seele quält.

O Hoffnung lass durch dich empor gehoben,

den Dulder ahnen, dass dort oben,
ein Engel seine Thränen zählt.

Thou who in night with festal splendor shining,
Renews life's beacon fire, declining,
And kindly veils the sufferer's fears;

Oh, hope! from thy bright sphere, to men discover
How full of love, thine angels hover over them
Recording their sad tears.

Beethoven's music is as poignant as the words. There are gorgeous chromatic half-steps from *"geho*ben*"* to *"den"* both times the line is sung (the second half of the stanza is repeated); the second time the phrase is one whole step lower in pitch than the first. There is an equally effective modulation under the second *"oben ein."* At times the accompaniment reminds one of the flowing right-hand figure of the opening movement of the piano sonata known as the *Moonlight* (Opus 27 No. 2).

As noted in the Introduction of this book a song cycle consists of several songs linked by the meaning of the texts, the key relationships of the settings, and the musical material itself. Although the cycle is thought of as an entity because the composer plots his contrasts and climaxes with the overall effect in mind, each of the songs usually has its own clearcut beginning, middle, and end, so one song *can* be excerpted if a performer insists. Beethoven's only song cycle, *An die ferne Geliebte (To the Distant Beloved),* the first genuine cycle encountered in the literature, is unique in that its six songs are joined by indispensable piano passages; none but the last comes to a real finish, although songs numbers 1 and 5 have fairly satisfactory closes.

The six texts are all love poems in a variety of moods—wistful, yearning, happy, melancholy, and so forth. We shall discuss only the first, which is in five strophically treated stanzas. The words describe a young man's thoughts as he roams over the mountains thinking of his beloved. He asks if she remembers the vows their hearts exchanged, and says that only song, "song that breathes of love's sweet pain," can ease his overflowing heart.

Beethoven uses the same simple melody over and over again in this song, but to avoid monotony he provides considerable ornamental variation in the accompaniment. The basic harmonic plan doesn't change, but the piano figurations do. One salient example is the diminished chord found in the sixth measure of the melodic line: sometimes it is made more powerful by the use of a suspension (one note from outside the chord which gives a dissonance until it resolves to the "right" note) and sometimes it is not. The melody itself is strongly rooted in the tonic scale of the piece, E flat major for high voice.

Despite Beethoven's inventiveness in varying the accompaniment, and despite the tender and moving quality of the melodic line, the repetitiousness does become somewhat wearing. In fact this is the criticism most frequently voiced of Beethoven's longer songs. In the cycle as a whole the beautiful modulations between songs—especially between one and two and two and three—revive interest. The music of this first song returns as an epilogue to the last, completing the cycle.

"Der Kuss" brings us back to Beethoven in a lighter mood, although extremists in the women's movement might not find it amusing. The little poem, by Weisse, has a swaggering young man bragging of his conquest of Chloë. He tells her that he will kiss her; she says if he does she'll scream. He kisses her anyway and does she scream? Oh, yes, but later—*much* later! Beethoven's naive Haydnesque setting of this bit of braggadocio nullifies the macho quality of the words, for all is youthful innocence and high spirits. It is heartwarming to hear this bit of fluff from the great composer just as he was about to reach his last creative period, the years of his most difficult, thorny, and sublime works.

Lesser Known German Composers Before Schubert

The songs of several lesser-known composers of this period were popular enough in their day to warrant brief mention in this study. From Mozart's generation we list Johann Schulz (1747–1800) and Johann Hiller (1728–1804), both of whom brought lively musical imaginations to the strophic "Volkslied" or folk-song form. The works of three slightly later composers, Karl Friedrich Zelter (1758-1823), Johann Reichardt (1752-1814), and Johann Zumsteeg (1760-1802) had a considerable influence on the earlier songs of Franz Schubert. Interestingly enough Zelter and Reichardt both set Goethe's "Der Erlkönig" to music at about the same time as Schubert; only Schubert's setting—one of his earliest masterpieces— remains in the repertoire.

Contemporaneous with Schubert (1797-1828) are three other song composers who are still familiar to concertgoers: Karl Maria von Weber (1786–1826), Louis Spohr (1784–1859), and Karl Loewe (1796–1869). Spohr is represented on the concert stage today principally by his octet, a lively, charming composition for double string quartet, and by his six German Songs, Opus 103, for soprano, clarinet, and piano. The sound combination of clarinet and female voice is a most winning one; Schubert was to use it to much greater effect in his delightful "Der Hirt auf dem Felsen." The Spohr songs, while charming and ingratiating, seem to lack vigor and pall after several hearings. Nevertheless the ingenuous "Wiegenlied" ("Lullaby") and "Zwiegesang" ("Two Songs in One") in which the three parts are particularly beautifully intertwined, make the set a valued part of the very limited repertoire for this beguiling combination.

Karl Maria von Weber was the strongest composer of the three and is by far the best represented on the current scene. His operas *Der Freischütz* and *Oberon* show his considerable gifts for orchestration; his virtuosic piano solo *The Invitation to the Dance* is full of original harmonic ideas and demanding figurations (he was a brilliant pianist); his clarinet concerti and solo pieces are indispensable staples of the clarinet literature, and his trio for flute, cello, and piano is the best work extant for that combination.

Although his songs do not show him at his best, many are pleasant and a few exhibit the sparks of originality that give his more important works lasting appeal. In the six songs of Opus 23, for instance, the second ("Rhapsodie") has a striking minor chord in the sixth bar. Its overall rhythmic plan—a very slow beginning, an abrupt shift to allegro, and a gradual ritard until the slow tempo of the opening is reached at the end—seems to give this very brief song much more scope than its length would indicate. The third song of the set has an interesting raised note in the melody; the tune consists of all the notes of the C major scale except D, but instead of F, Weber gives an F sharp. Further along in the piece there is an unexpected one-and-a-half-step interval (from G sharp to F natural and back to G sharp) in the melody. Since this song can be accompanied by either guitar or piano, the accompaniment is simple and features strummed repeated chords; nevertheless it is interesting and imaginative throughout. (Weber wrote many songs with guitar instead of piano accompaniments.)

The third of Schubert's contemporaries, Karl Loewe, is the least known internationally, but his ballads are still sung in his native Germany and occasionally appear on recital programs elsewhere. It is no surprise that he too wrote music for Goethe's "Der Erlkönig," for it was just this sort of melodramatic story that appealed to him; of the 368 songs credited to him, most are ballads to texts of a similar or even more Gothic nature. Loewe's setting of "Der Erlkönig" is far less tempestuous than Schubert's, for the Erlking, the Angel of Death, lures the lad tenderly, and the father speaks gently. In lieu of the constantly storming octaves and raging bass passages of the Schubert piece, Loewe gives us a light tinkling piano figuration to depict the elves the boy sees. The three characters, the frightened boy, the laconic father, and the Erlking himself, are well differentiated in the music, and the tragic end is forceful and dramatic.

Although some of Loewe's ballads tend to sound overblown—one is sometimes reminded of music for silent movies—many are gripping for both their stories and their music. Two examples of Loewe's songs including "Der Erlkönig" can be heard on *The Seraphim Guide to German Lieder* (SIC 6072).

In addition to the composers mentioned here, there are of course many whose names are now too seldom encountered to warrant inclusion in this by no means exhaustive study. Occasionally one will come across a fine song by an unknown composer who was momentarily inspired by a poem or a situation to rise above his own limitations. These are added delights for the enterprising recitalist or amateur.

From Schubert through Schoenberg the great masters of

German art song—Schumann, Brahms, Wolf, Strauss, Mahler, and Berg—so overshadow their contemporaries that we shall focus our study only on these giants, bearing in mind always that we thereby slight many a beautiful song.

Franz Schubert
(1797–1828)

Music teachers tell the following—one hopes apocryphal—story: in response to a question on a music appreciation exam a student wrote, "The famous 'Three B's' of music are Bach, Beethoven, and Mozart." One can understand the student's aesthetic judgment if not his orthography, but what then about the phenomenon known as Schubert? Whenever potential chamber-music audiences are polled as to their favorite work, the result is inevitably a victory for Schubert's *Trout Quintet;* ask piano-trio players which work in their repertoire they consider the most beautiful and odds are they'll name the slow movement of Schubert's B flat Trio, Opus 99; pianists who know the four-hand literature find no rival for Schubert's F minor Fantasy or Opus 35 Variations; and as yet we have not even mentioned the astounding body of over six hundred songs with which Schubert created the core of the German art song. There is no doubt that Schubert, the source of a boundless stream of beautiful melodies, of delightfully original harmonic turns, and of the most evocative atmospheric settings, is among the greatest composers of all time, and that the art song was for him the most natural and immediate form of expression.

This brings us to the problem of choice, for it is clear

that we cannot even mention more than a sampling of his songs in a survey of this nature. In an attempt to provide an overview, we have selected his first two published songs, Opus 1 and Opus 2, "Der Erlkönig" and "Gretchen am Spinnrade"; two fairly early single songs, "Die Forelle" of 1817 and "Auf dem Wasser zu singen" of 1823; one song from the 1823 cycle *Die Schöne Müllerin* ("Wohin?"); three songs from the later (1827) cycle "Winterreise" ("Der Lindenbaum," "Die Post," and "Der Leiermann"); and three songs written in 1828, the last year of his life, "Ständchen," "Der Doppelgänger," and "Der Hirt auf dem Felsen." Most of these songs are well-known favorites, but so are many others—"Heidenröslein," "Der Wanderer," "Der Tod und das Mädchen," "Geheimnis," "An die Musik," and "Ganymed," to name but a few. No suggestions re recordings seem necessary since the great Schubert interpreters such as Dietrich Fischer-Dieskau, Hans Hotter, and Hermann Prey are well represented on major labels, but special mention might be made of the Columbia record (MS–6236) on which Benita Valente sings "Der Hirt auf dem Felsen" with the collaboration of pianist Rudolf Serkin and clarinetist Harold Wright.

"Gretchen am Spinnrade" or "Gretchen at the Spinning Wheel," although published as Opus 2, was written the year before "Der Erlkönig," which is numbered Opus 1. Actually publishers assigned opus numbers to Schubert's works with very little regard to chronology, early works receiving late opus numbers if, as was so often the case, they were not published until years after their completion. In this case the exact date of composition, October 19, 1814, is of interest because "Gretchen" is among Schubert's earliest acknowledged masterpieces. The psychological understanding his music evinces of this distraught young girl who is about to be seduced by Faust is all the more remarkable when one real-izes that Schubert had not yet reached his eighteenth birth-day when he wrote it.

From the song's first introductory measure one is aware of Schubert's highly original concept of the function of the accompaniment in an art song, for the piano plays an inde-pendent part in the telling of the story by simulating the whirring sound of a spinning wheel. This onomatopoeic fig-uration goes on ceaselessly while the girl sings of her dis-tress: "Meine Ruh ist hin, mein Herz ist schwer" ("My peace is gone, my heart is heavy"). The melody is restless and agitated over the droning piano; the mode is minor as befits the troubled words. As the maiden reflects on "His lofty stance, his noble figure, his smile, the force of his gaze," the music subtly shifts to the major mode. Her remin-iscence is almost trancelike and the accompaniment is ever more hypnotic until she suddenly recalls "sein Kuss" ("his kiss"). At the climactic words the high G in the melody and the piano's diminished chord abruptly break the spinning thread and the girl's fantasy. While the voice is momentarily silent the piano figuration imitates two unsuccessful at-tempts to start the spinning wheel in motion again. Finally on the third try, the hypnotic whirring recommences, and the voice enters with the final verses.

The form of the song is sui generis.* The repeated use of the opening melodic phrase for the beginning of stanzas 2, 4 (the fourth stanza is a repeat of the words of the first, in-serted by Schubert), 5, and 8 (another reprise of the words of stanza 1) gives a strophic effect, but only the music for the thrice-heard words of the opening stanza is really repeated.

---

*Although the Schubertian trademark of a piano prelude and post-lude is already in evidence.

The music for the other verses varies according to the demands of the text, the rise toward "sein Kuss" in the middle and the almost hysterical high A's in the last verse being obvious examples. The song ends with a pathetic reprise of the opening words, "Meine Ruh ist hin, mein Herz ist schwer," once again to the same plaintive melodic line and whirring accompaniment. The vocal line more or less breaks off on the dominant while the spinning wheel goes on for a few more moments. The effect is one of complete emotional exhaustion.

In 1815, the year after "Gretchen," Schubert wrote 145 songs, 30 of them to texts by Goethe. Best known of that remarkable group is "Der Erlkönig." Once again the piano begins with a figuration important to the story, this time insistent triplet octaves depicting the galloping horse. These octaves present a big problem for the pianist, for they require tremendous strength and endurance. Periodically the left hand has a stormy rising figure against the right hand's octaves, which adds to the tension.

The singer must portray four separate characters in this drama—the frightened young boy, the protective father, the sometimes enticing, sometimes menacing Erlking (obviously the Angel of Death), and the narrator who opens and closes the scene. The Erlking has his own accompanying figures— light, rather neutral chords or broken chords instead of the galloping octaves—when he speaks sweetly to the boy. In his final verse, when he tells the boy that if he doesn't come willingly he will use force, he too is accompanied by the wildly driving octaves.

The song's frenzy, which one senses from the opening measure, continues unabated until the chilling last line, "In seinem Armen das Kind war tot" ("In his arms the child was dead"). For this conclusion the piano ceases its clatter and the words stand out in bold relief. Two simple chords, the dominant and the tonic, end the doleful song. For sheer energy and drama this song is unsurpassed.

Nothing could be more different in mood than the charming little "Die Forelle" ("The Trout"), whose irresistible melody Schubert used in the theme and variations movement of the so-called *Trout Quintet** (Opus 114), which he composed in 1819, two years after the song. The text, by a minor poet named Schubart, tells the story of a trout who sees the bait at the end of the fisherman's rod, but is too smart to touch it. In desperation the fisher muddies the water and the trout, no longer able to see the rod, grabs the bait and is caught. Once again it is the piano that captures in sound the burbling brook and the quickly darting trout. The vocal line is blithe, gay, and as natural as a folk tune. When the fisher decides on his deceitful ploy, the accompaniment becomes wittily melodramatic, with menacing diminished chords and minor intervals; when the trout is finally caught, the piano comments with breathless pauses and ominous chords. The poem ends sadly, "und ich mit regem Blute sah die Betrog'ne an" ("And I watched with blood astir the betrayed one"), but the music returns to the insouciance of the beginning as though the trout had gotten away.

"Auf dem Wasser zu singen," Schubert's Opus 72, may be translated "To be Sung on the Waters." It is yet another example of an extraordinary accompanying figuration which whirls around the vocal line in imitation of flowing water. Schubert seemed to have an endless stock of pianistic patterns suggestive of babbling brooks and swirling eddies. Never reluctant to repeat a phrase or line of verse when the music seemed to call for it, Schubert took even greater than usual liberties with this mediocre poem by the little-known

---

*Scored for violin, viola, cello, double bass, and piano.

poet Stolberg, repeating some couplets and some single lines to satisfy the strophic structure.

Some of Schubert's stylistic trademarks are very much in evidence in this song. First is the free-flowing melodic line given to the voice. Schubert's melodies almost always convey this spontaneous fluidity; like this one they seem entirely natural, lending themselves effortlessly to repetition and variation. The piano's figure is similar to and yet quite distinctive from the vocal line. The two, while maintaining their individuality, blend harmonically, creating the feeling of a duet rather than of soloist and accompanist. Interestingly enough, the piano is almost always above the voice in pitch. Schubert was a brilliant harmonist, and the skill with which he manipulates the two voices so that they are sometimes in thirds, sometimes in fifths or sixths, and occasionally in seconds or sevenths, elevates this music way above the ordinary obbligato harmonization so common in vocal music.

Another Schubertian characteristic found in this song is the constant shifting from minor to major. Although the key signature indicates A flat major as the main key (for high voice), the opening measures are in A flat minor; from this key Schubert slips down a third to F flat major—another favorite device. It is not until the third measure before the piano postlude, in other words when the song is almost over, that we find ourselves in the A flat major tonic. All kinds of fascinating modulations have of course intervened, many revolving around intervals of a third (from E flat [7] to C flat in bars 4 and 5 after the voice enters, or from C flat major to A flat minor six bars later, for example). Schubert is the master of the unexpected modulation, and somehow the surprises remain fresh after dozens of hearings.

Both cycles composed by Schubert, *Die Schöne Müllerin (The Sweet Maid of the Mill)* and *Winterreise (Winter's Journey)*, use competent but uninspired texts by a poet named Müller. This fact has led to the oft-repeated judgment that mediocre poems, since by definition they show some lack, make the best texts for art songs, for then the music can supply whatever element was missing. A reminder that some of Schubert's finest songs are settings of the great works of Goethe should dispel that myth—a great song to a second-rate text is great despite, not because of, the words.

Müller is the German word for miller, leading to the surmise that the story behind the collection of poems called *Die Schöne Müllerin* is autobiographical. The early poems are full of joy, as the young miller wanders over the beautiful countryside in lovely spring weather seeking his fortune. He asks the little brook he follows "Wohin?" ("Where are we going?") assuming that such an active brook will lead him to a mill. Indeed it does, and the miller has a beautiful daughter who reciprocates his ardor, and all is bliss. Suddenly a handsome hunter appears. The fickle young girl abandons the miller for the exciting hunter and the miller sadly leaves, carrying the withered flowers of their former love. There are twenty songs in the cycle, each expressing a stage in the story—anticipation, hope, ardor, joy, jealousy, heartache, despair, and finally death.

The second song of the cycle, "Wohin?" is full of youthful exuberance. Once again the accompaniment depicts a brook with its lively, gushing currents, but this time the mode is predominantly major and the figure is composed of simple broken triads. The melody is as much like a folk tune as a composed melody can hope to be, and its many repetitions give the song an ingenuous charm. Since the young miller is briskly walking beside the brook as he sings, the rhythm is square enough for an unregimented march.

For the most part the miller's tune rides jauntily above the gurgling accompaniment, but periodically the pianist's left hand echoes the vocal line, providing a nice virile underpinning. The form is at once obvious and elusive, based on repetition, variation, and combinations thereof. For example, the music for the second couplet is a repeat of the first; the third couplet begins with a new melody but concludes the same way the first two did. Couplet 4 is a full repeat, couplet 5 entirely new, and couplet 6 a slight variation of couplet 5. These twelve opening lines are sufficiently interrelated to form section A, for at "Ist das denn meine Strasse?" ("Is this then my route?") we clearly have a much greater contrast. Never again do we hear the music of the opening in exactly the same form but the familiar ending of couplets 1 through 4 returns to conclude the song. Meanwhile the accompanying figure, never for a moment slackening, gives additional unity to the delightful song.

Winterreise begins emotionally where *Die Schöne Müllerin* ended, in a mood of bitter disappointment. "Nun ist die Welt so trübe" ("But now the world is dreary") says the first poem, for "Die Liebe liebt das Wandern" ("love likes to wander"). The very titles of the songs chill the heart— "Gefror'ne Thränen" ("Frozen Tears"), "Erstarrung" ("Benumbed"), "Einsamkeit" ("Solitude"), "Der Greise Kopf" ("The Gray Head"), "Täuschung" ("Illusion"). The only bright spots in the twenty-four-song cycle occur when the forlorn poet looks back upon happier days, as he does in "Der Lindenbaum" ("The Linden Tree").

This well-loved song, the fifth in the cycle, is in a gentle, pastoral mood. The piano has a beautiful, fluttery introduction—the breeze rustling the leaves, perhaps—which must be played with the utmost delicacy. Two measures before the voice enters, the piano stops its fluttering figure and sounds chords reminiscent of woodwinds, perhaps hunting horns.

The melodic line for the first section of this ABA song is so similar to German folk tunes that it is often mistaken for one. Its opening phrase is the tonic triad and it stays entirely within the tonic scale. While the voice is singing, the piano has a simple harmonic accompaniment, based primarily on parallel thirds, a stylistic characteristic of folk-song harmonization. When the first section, which describes the tree under whose shade the poet dreamed of love, has come to an end, the piano once again plays its rustling figure, but this time in the minor mode. This introduces the much sadder B section, in which the poet says he now must wander "in tiefer Nacht" ("in deepest night"). In the middle of the section the mode reverts to major as the poet's thoughts return to the past, but a reappearance of the piano's rustling figure sounds an ominous, chilling note over which the voice describes the "kalten Winde" (the "cold winds") which sped him on his way. The piano has a fairly long solo interlude in which its characteristic figure shifts chromatically over a dominant pedal point, finally arriving at the hornlike chords which ended the introduction. The final section, a recapitulation of the melody and harmonic outline of the opening but with an accompanying figure derived from the middle section, ends with the comforting murmur of the linden tree which seems to say "du fändest Ruhe dort" ("You will find peace here").

In "Die Post," the thirteenth song of the cycle, the poet hears the post horn signaling the arrival of the mailman's galloping horse. His heart leaps, but there will be no news for him; his poor heart grieves because his lost love will no longer send word to him. He aches to ask the postman if he has seen his love, but knows not if he will.

The song is in two main sections, the first major and the second minor, both of which are repeated in toto (ABAB form). The piano begins with a rhythmic figure (the meter is 6/8) depicting the galloping horse. On the third measure the piano's right hand begins a bugle-call pattern, the sound of the post horn. Even when the voice enters with its sad tale, the animated gallop continues in the accompaniment until the end of section A, when there is a sudden break and a measure of silence. The piano begins the B section with minor chords, but the galloping rhythm returns unchanged. Schubert brings back the major mode for the song's ending.

One of the functions of this song is to provide much-needed contrast to the many dreamier songs in the cycle. The agitation is valid in light of the story line, and most effective in the overall context of the cycle.

The text of the last song of *Winterreise*, "Der Leier-mann" ("The Organ Grinder"), is brief enough to quote in full. It has been interpreted as a description of madness caused by grief; it is surely a song of death, the ultimate song of death in a cycle that includes "Die Krähe" and "Der Weg-weiser" ("The Raven" and "The Signpost"). Schubert's preoccupation with death is manifest from his earliest songs ("Der Erlkönig") to his last.

Drüben hinter'm Dorfe steht ein Leiermann,
und mit starren Fingern dreht er, was er kann.
Barfuss auf dem Eise wankt er hin und her,
und sein kleiner Teller bleibt ihm immer leer.

Keiner mag ihn hören, Keiner sieht ihn an,
und die Hunde knurren um den alten Mann.
Und er lässt es gehen, alles wie es will,
dreht, und seine Leier steht ihm nimmer still.

Wunderlicher Alter, soll ich mit dir gehn?
Willst zu meinen Liedern deine Leier dreh'n?

Behind the village stands an organ-grinder
And with stiff fingers grinds as best he can.
Barefoot on the ice he wanders here and there,
No one hears him, no one sees him
And the dogs growl at the old man.
And he lets it all be, as it is;
Turns and the organ never stops.

Wonderful old one, shall I go with you?
Will you play my songs on your organ?

The music would be almost childlike in its simplicity were it not for its minor modality. The piano begins with the kind of open chords (the one and the five without the three of the scale) one hears from a street organ; these chords continue throughout the song, never changing key. In fact there is no harmonic motion of any kind in the piece—we have only tonic and dominant chords—making this unique among Schubert's songs.

The piano and singer alternate in presenting the sad chord-derived melodic line. The song's two stanzas are treated strophically, after which we have a brief coda and piano postlude. Little need be said about this heartbreaking song, for it makes its point so simply yet so eloquently. Unlike many of Schubert's songs, its accompaniment and vocal line are well within the grasp of the average amateur, but its interpretation requires great artistry.

Fourteen separate songs written by Schubert in the last year of his life have been grouped together by publishers under the title *Schwanengesang (Swan Song).* These songs do not constitute a song cycle as they are unrelated in poetry or music.

"Ständchen" or "Serenade" (the poem is by Rellstab) is probably the most familiar of these late works, for its melody has been arranged and rearranged by dozens of "popularizers." Despite its 3/4 rhythm it has the lilt of a barcarole or lullaby. Its accompaniment consists primarily of semide-tached chords reminiscent of the lute or guitar the nocturnal serenader might be strumming beneath his beloved's window. Occasionally the piano echoes the singer's phrase or joins in harmony. Interestingly enough when the piano and voice blend harmonically, the piano has the top pitch and the voice the accompanying one.

After two gentle strophic stanzas, there is an impassioned six-bar passage in which the poet expresses his fear of losing his love. The piano has two measures in which to calm the music down again and we then have an echo of the concluding phrases of the earlier stanzas. The song ends with a gently falling melodic line and the words "komm, beglücke mich" ("Come, bless me").

Of a far darker nature is "Der Doppelgänger," a German figure of speech invariably indicating the Shadow of Death. The meaning of the poem, a work of the great Heinrich Heine, is not absolutely clear: in a deserted street, in the still of night, the poet sees a man standing in front of the house of his long-dead beloved. He shudders to recognize his own face, his own form in "Du Doppelgänger, du bleicher Geselle" ("you double, you pale companion"). He asks, "was öffst du nach mein Liebeslied, das mich gequölt auf dieser Stelle?" ("Why do you mimic my love song, my painful tryst?"). No answer is forthcoming, but one senses horror and imminent death.

The piano begins the song with low-pitched funereal chords; the accompaniment never leaves the lower registers of the piano. The voice enters with a colorless note which is repeated for six consecutive syllables and to which the singer constantly returns (it is the dominant note, top of the triad, fifth note of the scale). The effect is deliberately monotonous, almost hypnotic. On the fifth line of verse the voice begins to rise, and a crescendo builds in the accompaniment. A crashing chord signals the climax of the phrase after which the voice drops an octave back to its original note. A similar rise to an even higher note brings a second climax and again a drop back to the opening pitch. Strangely enough, although there is no solace in words or music, Schubert ends the song on an unexpected major chord.

Since 1827 and 1828 saw the publication of so many sorrowful songs dealing with death and loss of love, some

biographers have felt that Schubert was expressing a pre-
monition of his tragically premature death (of all the famous
composers his thirty-one-year span is the shortest, save Pergolesi who died at the age of twenty-six). Nevertheless in
October, one month before his death, he wrote one of his
gayest, most exuberant songs, "Der Hirt auf dem Felsen"
("The Shepherd on the Rock"). This delightful salute to
spring is one of Schubert's most beloved pieces of chamber
music; its scoring for soprano, clarinet, and piano makes it
unique among his compositions. It may very well be the last
piece he ever wrote.

The poem, by the same Müller who contributed the texts
for the two great cycles, begins wistfully, as the shepherd
describes his loneliness away on the mountaintop, so far
from his home and his loved one. His voice echoes in the
empty hills. His gloom deepens for a while—he is so alone—
but suddenly spring is coming, "Der Frühling will kom-
men," and his voice rings out in happiness.

Since the piece is much longer than the average single
song, Schubert can afford to be expansive. He begins with a
long duet for clarinet and piano in which the clarinet introduces the melodies of the first section. From the beginning
there are echo effects which are used to even greater advantage when the voice joins in. The singer enters with an imitation of the clarinet's first melody; clarinet and voice then
alternate in presenting the melodic line, the piano having
minimal accompanying chords. After a while, for textural
variety, Schubert allows the piano to join the clarinet in echo
effects. Soon voice and clarinet overlap in their melodic lines,
another textural variation.

For the sadder center section Schubert shifts to the minor mode (from B flat major to its relative minor, G). He
subtly slows the sense of motion without real tempo change
by switching the accompanying chords from triplets to

eighth notes. The listener's heart aches in sympathy for the poor shepherd, his loneliness is so poignantly expressed in the music. A clarinet cadenza brings the section to a close and suddenly the mood changes completely. From G minor we return to B flat major; from a slow 3/4 time we move to an allegretto 2/4; and the melody, introduced once again by the clarinet, changes to a jaunty sixteenth-note scale fragment. As in the beginning the singer echoes the clarinet's line, and the two frolic together. A più mosso (a little faster) marking toward the end pushes the music to an even livelier pace. The singer's triumphant high B flat and the clarinet's virtuosic cadenza bring the music to a rousing close.

One hopes that Schubert's spirits were as high so near the end of his life as this sparkling song would indicate. Somehow the thought removes a bit of the sting of his pitifully early death.

Robert Schumann
(1810–1856)

Just as the art song was Franz Schubert's most natural form of musical expression, so the short, quasi-improvisational piano piece was Robert Schumann's innate approach to composition. His most successful piano works—*Papillons, Carnaval, Kinderscenen,* and *Kreisleriana*—are actually groups of brief atmospheric sketches held together by key relationships, cyclical themes, and interacting moods, with literary and musical allusions often used to provide additional unity to the loose structures.

If the above description of Schumann's technique of piano writing sounds awfully close to the formula for a song cycle, the similarity is far from coincidental. "Kreis" means cycle; Schumann wrote two song cycles (Opuses 24 and 39) entitled simply *Liederkreis*. In all Schumann composed five song cycles (the three others are *Myrthen,* Opus 25, *Frauen-liebe und Leben,* Opus 42, and *Dichterliebe,* Opus 48) and several sets of somewhat related songs to texts by a single poet, of which the most important are Opus 35 to twelve poems by Kerner, Opus 36 to six poems by Reinick, Opus 37 to twelve poems by Rückert, and Opus 98a, settings of nine poems from *Wilhelm Meister* by Goethe.

Obviously the solo song with piano accompaniment is very closely related to the short piano piece. Since Schumann's passion for literature was almost as great as his love for music, combining poetry with piano settings was a natural step for him; only in this genre do his works approach the spontaneity and certainty of his piano compositions.

Schumann was one of Schubert's greatest admirers. Biographers tell us that the eighteen-year-old lad wept the night through when he learned of Schubert's death. Largely as a result of this influence he had composed over a dozen songs before his nineteenth birthday, but a great spurt of pianistic inspiration drove all other thoughts from his mind from 1829 to 1840. He did begin work on several piano concerti, a symphony, and a string quartet during those years, but completed none of them; he was evidently too absorbed in "his" instrument. Many of his early piano pieces were also inspired by Schubert, especially the early polonaises for piano four-hands.

Suddenly, in 1840, triggered perhaps by the happy de-nouement to his well-known struggle for the hand of Clara Wieck, Schumann quite literally burst into song. The twelve-month period from February 1, 1840, to February 1, 1841, saw the birth of over 120 songs, including most of his finest. No one but Schubert has ever surpassed such a creative onslaught. Why he turned from piano to song at this time is a mystery; why he turned from song to symphony after the year is perhaps easier to explain: he thought it was his obligation to work on longer forms, and Clara, now his wife, agreed. Schumann did not totally abandon the song form after 1841, but it was not until 1850 that he returned to it with any intensity. While some of the late songs are very beautiful, it is really on the masterpieces of 1840–41 that his reputation as a songwriter rests.

Because Schumann thought so predominantly in terms of interlocking groups of songs, we shall concentrate our remarks on *Frauenliebe und Leben,* the eight-song cycle dealing with *The Love and Life of a Woman,* composed in 1840 to poems of Adelbert von Chamisso. We shall also discuss his famous ballad "Die beiden Grenadiere" and two brief songs from other cycles: "Mondnacht" from *Liederkreis* (Opus 39) and "Der Nussbaum" from *Myrthen* (Opus 25). All these songs are from that golden year 1840.

Although critics have taken Schumann to task for choosing the rather sentimental poems of Chamisso as the ideal expression of the emotions of a nineteenth-century woman, the beautiful melodies these texts inspired in the composer have made *Frauenliebe und Leben* one of his best-loved works. *Dichterliebe (The Poet's Love),* to which *Frauenliebe und Leben* is usually unfavorably compared, has the undeniable advantage of Heinrich Heine's veiled poetry, which released music of great psychological depth in Schumann. These psychological insights are expressed in the delicate, subtle harmonic touches with which the cycle abounds. The more straightforward, homely emotions of Chamisso's poems, on the other hand, evoked from the composer some of his warmest, most sensual melodies. "Du Ring an meinem Finger," for instance, the fourth song in the cycle, may be one of the most singable tunes in the art song literature.

The cycle begins with three simple chords from the piano. The significance of these chords, with their suggestive rhythmic pattern (there is a hesitation before the third chord which connotes expectancy, timidity), is greatly enlarged by their reappearance at the beginning of the piano's epilogue, with which the cycle closes. Throughout the first song, "Seit ich ihn gesehen" ("Since I Have Seen Him"), which describes the young girl's adoration of her beloved, the rhythmic patterns are highly expressive, especially in the measures in which the piano's quarter-note chord occurs on the second half of the second beat (measure 4 under "blind zu sein," for example). Here the feeling is one of a precipitous leap—as though her heart has skipped a beat. The melody begins timidly with very small intervals, but soars romantically under "wie im wachen Traume" ("as in a waking dream"). The two verses are treated strophically and the piano closes with an extended presentation of the opening chords.

The second song is forceful and exuberant, as she describes him, "The Most Glorious of All" (Er, der Herrlichste von allen"). This is one of the poems most criticized for its false sentiment, for in the middle section she says that she hopes he won't notice her. She is too humble; he must seek only the worthiest and she will be content to look at him from afar even if her heart should break. The poem ends with the lines "Brich, o Herz, was liegt daran?" ("Break, oh, heart, what does it matter?").

Whatever one thinks of the sentiment, the girl's confused and agitated thoughts are beautifully expressed in the music. The melody begins with a falling and then rising tonic triad while the piano beats time with the same chord. The piano echoes part of the vocal line canonically and repeats the melody's most characteristic phrase in the interludes. Constantly modulating harmonies characterize the third stanza of this through-composed song whose form may be roughly outlined as AAB for the first half, but whose second half follows the dictates of the words in a less easily discerned pattern. The final verse is a repeat of the A music but in a lower key. The piano's epilogue introduces new material, a stylistic device invented by Schumann, which comments sadly on the closing words.

"Ich kann's nicht fassen, nicht glauben" ("I cannot grasp or believe it"), says the third song, for he has chosen her above all others. Instead of joy the music expresses bewilderment, even fear, the piano's first series of detached chords culminating in a held diminished chord. The key is minor and the form ABA, but when the da capo section is over, instead of stopping, the song continues with a wonderful coda in which the mood completely changes. The piano abandons its staccato chords for a gently rocking melody; the voice reenters with repeated tonic notes, finally rising a fourth while the piano's melodic line rises above it to the octave. The last three measures, once again a piano postlude, are in blissful major, telling us that somehow her fears have been allayed. If the music is psychologically more insightful than the words, so be it.

The outstanding feature of the next song, "Du Ring an meinem Finger" ("You Ring on my Finger") is its wonderful melody. For the most part the piano doubles the singer's line, occasionally providing little countermelodies in the bass. In the middle section, which is marked "nach und nach rascher" ("more and more excited"), the girl's increasing excitement is expressed by the chromatically rising melodic line and the agitated accompanying chords, but the sensuously rounded melody returns to end the song. In this case the piano's epilogue is a continuation of the main material of the song.

"Helft mir, ihr Schwestern" ("Help Me, My Sisters") is

all happy excitement, as the bride prepares for the wedding. The music is quite reminiscent of one of Schumann's slightly earlier songs, "Widmung," from Opus 25 (still 1840 but earlier in the year). The piano begins the song with a rising and then falling arpeggio, marked by a dotted rhythm at the end of each measure. The song is in rondo form, AABB' AACC'A, but again there is a mood-changing coda for the last two lines. The poem ends "But you sisters, I greet with sadness, / Joyfully parting from your midst." The music responds to this hint of wistfulness with an abrupt modulation, a ritard, and a very gentle sound. The major mode remains, however, and the tempo quickens after a brief two measures, as joy chases away even the slightest ambivalence. The piano postlude is a reference to Wagner's famous Wedding March—Schumann loved musical as well as literary allusions—which blends with the song's own thematic material.

The two poems most difficult to accept in light of twentieth-century mores are the sixth, "Susser Freund" ("Sweet Friend") and "Nun Hast du Mir den Ersten Schmerz Getan" ("Thus You Have Caused Me the First Pain"), the last of the cycle. In "Susser Freund" the shy young matron cannot find words modest enough with which to tell her husband that she is pregnant. Her tears are tears of rapture, her heart is throbbing. Finally she says that she will place a cradle near her bed and the morning will come when "der Traum erwacht" ("the dream awakens") and *his* image will smile up at her from the cradle. If these words seem farfetched in an era when people discuss their most intimate affairs at dinner parties, the music—tender, hesitant, full of wonder and warmth—is far from dated.

The piano begins with expanding chords, and the voice enters with a falling melodic interval. The two parts overlap, the piano beginning its phrase anew while the singer is completing her musical thought. The opening melodic phrase is heard four times in the first section, with contrasting phrases for the third, fourth, seventh, and eighth lines of verse. The B section in this essentially AABA song is characterized by increased excitement as melody and accompaniment rise chromatically, the piano now playing agitated detached chords. The most affirmative music occurs to the words "Bleib' an meinem Herzen, fühle dessen Schlag" ("Stay near my heart, feel its throbbing"). An accelerando describes her mounting passion as she clasps him firmer and firmer, the heartbeat chords going faster and faster. Suddenly long chords in the accompaniment calm the music and we return to the tenderness of the opening section. For the first time in the cycle the voice participates in the epilogue, singing "dein Bildnis" ("Your image") over the last chord in the piano part.

Maternal love is the subject of the seventh song, "An meinem Herzen, an meiner Brust" ("On My Heart, on My Breast"). Once again the melody is joyous and exhilarating. The piano's part is a swirling sixteenth-note figure which busily surrounds the vocal line. For the last verse the accompaniment switches to staccato chords, primarily to allow an even faster tempo for the singer—the last verse is marked "noch schneller" ("still faster"). There is a ritard at the last few words which is continued by the piano in the epilogue. As in the second and sixth songs of the cycle, new material is introduced in the piano postlude, this time perhaps to provide a better link between the unmitigated joy of this song and the profound sorrow of the next.

The last song of *Frauenliebe und Leben* is a brief one. The husband has died and the widow is in turn bitter ("Thus you have caused me the first pain . . . you hard and cruel man") and disconsolate ("The world is empty . . . I do not live anymore"). While it is true that the majority of women survive widowhood and go on with their own fruitful lives, surely these sentiments must be common among the newly bereaved even today, and the criticism of Chamisso exaggerated.

The stark music is based on a minor triad, first struck as a chord on the piano and then echoed in melodic intervals by the voice. Dissonances caused by suspensions make the music even bleaker, as does the narrow melodic line with its many declamatory repeated notes. The vocal part ends on a note from the dominant chord, leaving the cycle unfinished, so to speak. A beautiful modulation in the piano brings us back to the key of the opening song, which the piano then repeats in its entirety (one complete verse, that is) without the vocal part. Thus is the cycle completed. Any doubt that for Schumann the song is an extension of the short piano piece is dispelled on hearing this "accompaniment" which is quite complete on its own.

In an attempt to compose longer dramatic works (he worked unsuccessfully on several opera projects, finally completing *Genoveva* in 1850), Schumann set many narrative ballads to music. Although this was really not his forte, one very popular song resulted, the familiar "Die beiden Grenadiere." In this extremely patriotic song two French soldiers are wending their way home from Russia after Napoleon's defeat. The music is a slow, somber march, indicating sorrow and despair which cannot completely obliterate military discipline. The structure is loosely strophic with stanzas 1, 3, and 5 sung to the defiant, angry material, and alternate stanzas much more plaintive. The accompaniment is constantly changing to express the varying moods. For the last two stanzas Schumann uses the music of France's national anthem, "La Marseillaise," a rousing martial tune if ever there was one, but a sad epilogue destroys the pitiful bravura of the heartbroken grenadiers. Some critics hear parody in the epilogue, claiming that the song is tongue in cheek, but this interpretation seems capricious.

"Mondnacht" ("Moonlit Night") and "Der Nussbaum" ("The Walnut Tree"), two short but exquisite songs, are excellent examples of Schumann's two basic styles of song-writing. The former has a luscious sensual melody in the vocal part and, with the exceptions of the piano prelude, postlude, and interludes, a very simple chordal accompaniment; the latter has a delicate melodic line which is more consistently present in the piano part, although the voice often participates. The piano part to "Der Nussbaum" would make a perfectly acceptable solo piano piece; the piano part to "Mondnacht" would be, for the most part, just an accompaniment in search of a tune.

Both poems speak of love, Schumann's favorite subject for a song, and both evoke nature as witness to and background for this human emotion. "Mondnacht" begins with a lovely lyric piano prelude, after which repeated notes introduce its soaring melody. This vocal line, which arches over a complete couplet, is heard twice. The entire section, prelude and twice-told melody, is then repeated. Only the penultimate couplet has a different melody, with the original vocal line returning, albeit with a downward rather than a rising ending, for the last two lines. The piano concludes the song with an even more serene postlude.

A comparison of Schumann's "Der Nussbaum" with Schubert's "Der Lindenbaum" points out some interesting differences between the two composers. Although Schumann's piano figuration suggests the delicate movement of flowery branches, Schubert's rustling figure is more onomatopoeic, actually sounding like the breeze fluttering through the leaves. While the Schumann song tells of whispered sighs and dreams of happiness, the Schubert song ranges in emotion from nostalgia to despair. "Der Nussbaum" is as complete a solo piece as any Mendelssohn "Song Without Words"; Schubert's piano part is in turn soloist and accompanist. The Schubert melody closely resembles a folk tune, while Schumann's is far too complex to be anything but a professionally composed vocal line.

There is a risk in drawing generalized conclusions from these isolated examples, but both songs are quite typical of their composers. Neither suffers by comparison, for each is ineffably beautiful in its own way.

Felix Mendelssohn

(1809–1847)

Since his premature death in 1847, there has been constant critical vacillation regarding the music of Felix Mendelssohn. Adored by musicians and music lovers during his lifetime, he has since been accused of shallowness, banality, and "sickly religiosity,"* yet his major works—the five Symphonies, the Overture and Incidental Music to *Midsummer Night's Dream*, the Octet for strings, the Violin Concerto, the D minor and C minor Piano Trios, the Oratorio *Elijah*, and so forth—have never left the standard repertoire.

It is true that some of the shorter pieces for piano solo— played to death by virtuosi two or three generations ago—are now somewhat out of favor, but to demote them to the realm of "salon music," as so many critics have, seems overharsh in light of their verve and élan. As for the songs, as might be expected considering their number (seventy-five solo and twelve duets), they vary: some might be dismissed as con-

---

Grove's Dictionary, Fifth Edition, vol. VII, p. 942.

ventional efforts, but many, while not really breaking any new musical ground, are lovely indeed.

Mendelssohn's best-known song, "Auf Flügeln des Gesanges" ("On Wings of Song," Opus 34 No. 2) is typical of his songwriting style. It has a beautiful, graceful, eminently singable melody, which flows along undisturbed by dissonance or rhythmic irregularity. Its structure is semistrophic, the music of the first verse repeated for the second and varied for the third. The accompaniment is an unending series of broken chords, the first two notes of which are held to enrich the sound. There is much emphasis on the main key (A flat) and those closely related to it, with a brief chromatic passage in the third verse to emphasize the climactic arrival at the high E flat on the word "Traum" ("dream"). The text, an exotic poem by Heine, invites the loved one to come away, on wings of song, to a garden on the banks of the Ganges, where lotus flowers bloom in the moonlight.

With the exception of the Nazis, to whom Mendelssohn, despite his conversion to Christianity, remained a Jew and therefore worthy of complete contempt, even his most severe critics have admired Mendelssohn's ability to create fantastic, dancing scherzi. This unique gift is reflected in the accompaniments of several of the songs, including "Neue Liebe" ("New Love," Opus 19 No. 4) and "Hexenlied" ("Witches' Song," Opus 8 No. 8).

"Neue Liebe" begins with light, scampering piano introduction in which one can almost hear the elves riding through the moonlit woods. The melody is at once mysterious and whimsical, its minor tonality (F sharp minor in the original key) providing the mystery, its dotted rhythm and staccato delivery providing the whimsy. The elves' horns, bells, and tiny white horses are described in the music, as the lovely text by Heine continues to elaborate on the enchanting scene. Finally the Queen of the Elves appears; she alone smiles and nods. Suddenly, midway through the third verse, the scherzolike piano part comes to a halt, and solemn chords accompany the text: "Galt das meiner neuen Liebe?/ Oder soll es Tod bedeuten?" ("Does that indicate my new love/ Or does it mean death?"). Before the singer has finished these ominous words, the piano resumes its fleet figuration, but a shadow of fear remains over the scherzo ending.

"Hexenlied" is all agitation and fairy-tale scariness. The first verse (poem by Ludwig Hölty) begins with a description of spring's swallows, flowers, and glorious dance. The climactic high note on *"Tanze"* ("dance") is accompanied by a tonic major chord (G minor is the main key) but on the second syllable of *"Tanze"* the piano begins a furious rush of minor scales, and the words speak of black goats and broomsticks. The second verse, to the same music as the first, introduces the malevolent Beelzebub (the devil) with his clawlike hands and insidious promises of riches. In the final verse, which begins like the other two but goes on to new material before returning to the original ending, a fiery dragon flies overhead frightening the neighbors. Excited tremolos in the accompaniment express fear and agitation. Wild octaves and arpeggios support the melodic climax, which rises to a high B flat, as the words return to "prächtigen Tanze" ("the glorious dance"). This is a wonderful accompaniment in Mendelssohn's best piano style.

Another example of a Mendelssohn song with a furiously virtuosic accompaniment is "Reiselied," or "Traveling Song" (Opus 34 No. 6). The mood of the song alternates from disconcerting drama to tranquillity, as the words (text by Heine) describe in turn autumn winds on a cold, damp night (foreboding music), the traveler's thoughts of his beloved (calm and joy), barking dogs (agitation and fear), and visions of his loved one waiting for him (peace and happiness). The final section is ominous indeed, as the oak tree asks through the howling wind, "What do you mean by this foolish dream?"

In a far gentler mood is the charming "Hirtenlied" ("Shepherd's Song," Opus 57 No. 2, text by Johann Uhland). One simple melody, based on the tonic triad, is heard throughout the song, in minor when the shepherd describes winter which confines everyone to his own little hut, in major when he envisions glorious summer when he can take his beloved to the mountain peaks where no one can see them. Like the text, the music is tender and naive.

Mendelssohn composed eight songs with the word "Frühling" ("spring") in the title, five of them called simply "Frühlingslied" ("Song of Spring"). As might be expected these songs are predominantly gay and sprightly. "Altdeutsches Frülingslied" ("Old German Spring Song," Opus 86 No. 6) is no exception—its rippling accompaniment and flowing melody gladden the heart. However the last four lines of its poem (by Spee) speak of pain and loss of love, and these sentiments are of course reflected in the music. Mendelssohn wrote this song one month before his death.

"Schilflied" ("Reed Song," Opus 71 No. 4, text by Nikolaus Lenau) possesses unusual depth for a Mendelssohn song. The poem is merely a description of a night scene—a motionless pond surrounded by garlands of reeds. Nevertheless these words inspired a melody of great poignancy, of quiet melancholia. Here the accompaniment is minimal, just harmonic background for the lovely words and melody.

Among Mendelssohn's most appealing vocal compositions are his duets Opus 63 Nos. 1–6. Written for two high voices, they are usually sung by two sopranos, although there is no real reason that they mightn't be done by soprano and tenor. The second, third, and fifth songs of the set are sweet, tender, and a bit on the sentimental side, but "Herbstlied" ("Autumn Song," No. 4) is more exciting, and "Maiglöckchen und die Blümelein" ("The Maybell and the Flowers," No. 6), is a delightful scherzando patter song. Five of the six texts are by German poets—Heine (No. 1), Hoffmann von Fallersleben (Nos. 2 and 6), Baron Joseph von Eichendorff (No. 3), and Karl Klingemann (No. 4) —but the fifth song, "Volkslied" ("Folk Song") is a translation of a poem by Robert Burns.

The only criticisms one might make of the set are that the voices tend to sing in thirds too much of the time, and changes of mood in the poems—sorrow at the end of "Abschiedslied der Zugvögel" ("Farewell Song of the Birds of Passage," No. 2), for instance—are not reflected in the music. Nevertheless these duets, known collectively as *Zweistimmige Lieder,* more than compensate in charm for whatever they lack in depth.

Johannes Brahms

(1833–1897)

By the time Johannes Brahms reached maturity, the art song had become a well-established tradition in Germany. Critics and connoisseurs were wont to measure the worth of new songs by comparison to the best of Schubert, a standard few were to achieve. Brahms, with his love of the traditional, studied Schubert's songs assiduously, and despite his fierce individuality, the imprint of Schubert's style may be found in many of the younger composer's vocal works.

Another strong influence on Brahms was Robert Schumann. Brahms first visited Robert and Clara Schumann in 1853 when he was still impressionable enough to absorb the stylistic characteristics of more mature composers. This visit resulted in a lifelong friendship between Clara and Brahms. Robert, who was already ill, died not quite three years after Brahms was introduced to the family, but Clara continued to advise and criticize the maturing composer. We therefore find in quite a few of his songs backgrounds in the Schumannesque style of piano writing.

Brahms was an enormously prolific songwriter. Only Schubert, the all-time champion, eclipses his output of two hundred solo songs, seventy folk-song settings, twenty-five duets, and over thirty vocal quartets with piano accompaniment, including the two sets of *Liebeslieder Waltzes,* both of which are long song cycles. Although there is great stylistic variety in his songs, certain characteristics pervade his vocal output: a tendency to choose poems describing love or nature within a rather narrow, somewhat bland emotional range (even of the *Four Serious Songs* of Opus 121, only the third reaches the depth of Schubert's most profound songs, although the gravely marching chords of the first song are quite imposing); an affinity for German folk tunes strong enough not only to provide material for his highly personal and imaginative folk-song settings but also to influence many of his original melodies; less concern with the purely literary aspect of his texts which sometimes leads to less than meticulous prosody; and a choice of tempi which tend to sound moderate whether they are marked allegro, andante, or adagio. Very often the accompaniments are composed of Schumannesque single-note figures which move freely around the vocal line while remaining in the background; seldom does one find the Schubertian piano figure which is supposed to imitate what the words describe. Of course to each of these generalities exceptions are easily found, but it is safe to say that for the most part Brahms is less turgid, less gruff, less pedantic, and more tender in his songs than in any other segment of his work save the late short piano pieces of

Opuses 116, 117, 118, 119, which have many songlike traits, and the G major and A major violin-piano sonatas (Opuses 78 and 100).

Like Schubert, Brahms expressed himself in song form throughout his life. Opuses 3, 5, and 7 (1851–53), composed before his first contact with Schumann, are his earliest published songs. There is no real hiatus in his song production, but 1868 was a banner year in which Opuses 43, 46, 47, 48, and 49—all songs—were published. (Opus 57, published three years later, was also probably composed in 1868.) The *Vier ernste Gesänge (Four Serious Songs* to biblical texts, Opus 121), written early in 1896, are among his last works, followed only by the eleven Organ Preludes of Opus 122.

We have chosen the following songs as representative of Brahms at various stages of his life: "Treue Liebe" from Opus 7 (1853 or earlier); "Die Mainacht" from Opus 43 (1868); "O wüsst' ich doch den Weg zurück" from Opus 63 (1873–74); "Geheimnis" from Opus 71 (1877); one of the three songs called "Mädchenlied"—Opus 85 No. 3 (1877–79), and two of the folk-song settings published in 1894 without opus number—"Mein Mädel hat einen Rosenmund" and "In stiller Nacht."

"Treue Liebe" ("True Love") is one of Brahms's earliest songs. Its poem, by Albert Dietrich, describes a maiden standing on the shore waiting in vain for her lover's return. As the waters play caressingly around her feet, she is drawn into the depths by a silent force. The last line says, "Sie hat den Geliebten gefunden!" ("She has found her beloved!").

The music begins quietly with the piano establishing the F sharp minor tonality (for high voice) with a figure that suggests swirling water. At this time Brahms's songs show the influence of Schubert who excelled in portraying various movements of water in musical terms. We find another typically Schubertian device a little later in the change from minor to major under "wie Träume" ("like dreams"). The melodic line shows much less motion than the accompaniment, underscoring the picture of the girl standing still while the waters eddy about her. The first two verses, treated strophically by Brahms, concentrate on the forlorn figure. In the third verse, where "Die Wasser unspielten ihr schmeicheln den Fuss" ("The water plays caressingly around her feet"), the melody starts out as though in repetition of the earlier verses while the motion of the water quickens (Brahms gives us triplet sixteenth notes instead of regular sixteenth notes to change the pace). A cascade of notes suggests the girl's being pulled out to sea and then beautiful exotic arpeggiated chords give the illusion of the vague beyond where she has rejoined her beloved. It's a hauntingly lovely song which shows originality in its harmonies despite its Schubertian overtones.

Poets often evoke nature to express human emotions. Perhaps the most poignant use of this time-honored device is to contrast man's loneliness and grief with nature's beauty. In "Die Mainacht" ("May Night") poet Ludwig Hölty does just that, describing the silver moon glistening on the trees, the nightingale singing, and—cruelest contrast of all—a pair of doves trilling of their rapture, while the protagonist seeks dark shadows in which to shed his lonely tears.

By the time this song was published, Brahms was in his mid-thirties. He had completed his great choral masterwork, the Requiem, which was at least partially inspired by his grief over the deaths of Schumann and his own mother. He was a man already acquainted with sorrow. His setting for this tender poem eschews obvious imitative devices—no trills in the piano part to portray the nightingale and only a subtle reference to the cooing of the doves under "Überhüllet vom Laub girret ein Taubenpaar." Instead there is a contemplative lyricism conveyed by the flowing melodic line and simple chordal accompaniment. When the poet speaks of the doves the tessitura* rises and the piano part becomes lighter. This makes the return to the bass register and heavier chords in the piano part under "aber ich wende mich" ("but I turn away") all the more effective in reestablishing the pain felt by the lonely poet.

Brahms provides variety in this essentially ABA song by changing the rhythm of the accompaniment for the da capo section. He intensifies the melodic line by allowing it to rise higher in the last section than it had in the first, the highest note of the comparable chromatic phrase occurring on the word "Trane" ("tear"). He then extends the section by having the melody rise again, this time even higher, before finally descending to the tonic note. The overall effect of the music is a gentle, philosophical sorrow which, despite its great beauty, does not quite match the anguish of the words.

"O wüsst' ich doch den Weg zurück" ("Oh, If Only I Knew the Way Back") is another wistful, melancholy text subtitled by its author, Klaus Groth, "Heimweh" ("Homesickness"). The words express the wish to return to the land of childhood, to find rest untroubled by strife, to be gently wrapped in love, to search no more, to be a child again, "ringsum ist öder Strand" ("for all about me is desolate shore")! The piano part consists primarily of octaves in the left hand and slowly arpeggiated chords in the right. Since the harmonies are in constant flux, one has the general impression of almost aimless wandering. At the beginning of the second stanza, "O wie mich sehne auszuruhn" ("Oh, how I long to rest"), the vocal line becomes highly chromatic and the accompaniment—for one brief measure—stops its wandering. At the second measure of this B section, the pi-

---

*The general overall range in pitch exclusive of atypical high or low notes.

ano's right hand harmonizes the vocal line while the left hand resumes its peregrinations. This pattern is repeated for the third stanza although the melody is changed slightly in the third and fourth bars. The fourth stanza closely resembles the first in words and music, the music matching the text in extent of variation. Although the music is far from gay, its major modality and the fact that the melody and harmonies find the home key at the end of both A sections (the form is ABBA) keep it from despair.

The message of "Geheimnis" is similar to that of Schumann's "Der Nussbaum," for the poet, Candidus, asks the trees why they stand so close to one another—are they whispering of our love? Unlike Schumann, however, Brahms makes no attempt to simulate the breeze ruffling the leaves. Instead he concentrates on the feeling of intimacy conveyed by the words, making of the vocal line and accompaniment the closest of duets.

The piano begins with gentle broken chords over a held and repeated tonic note. Immediately we sense intimacy because of the many overlapping notes and the interlocking harmonies. The voice's melodic line is of ineffable sweetness and without a trace of sentimentality. The piano stays discreetly in the background, occasionally incorporating the melody's notes in its right-hand phrases, for the first half of the song, after which it is allowed to share the melodic line with the singer. The charm of this serenely happy song fits poorly with Brahms's image as a feisty old curmudgeon!

To the confusion of listeners and performers alike, there are three Brahms songs with the same title, "A Maiden's Song" ("Mädchenlied"). These are settings of three different texts, one a translation by Siegfried Kapper of a Serbian poem, one an adaptation by Paul von Heyse of Italian words, and the last an original poem by Heyse. We shall discuss the first.

The Serbian poem (Opus 85 No. 3) tells of a maid who asks the rose why it blooms when she has no one for whom to pluck it—she is an orphan, her sister is long since married, her brother has gone to battle, and her lover is far away. The music is set in an unusual 5/4 rhythm, five quarter notes in each measure. To add to the complexity, in the initial piano figure, which later becomes part of the song proper, there is a typically Brahmsian two against three rhythmic pattern (eighth notes in the right hand, triplet eighths in the left). Brahms handles these complexities with such ease and naturalness that they seem simple and naive. Much later studies by Bartók and Kodály have proven that folk-dance music often features highly complex rhythmic patterns far removed from the oom-pah-pah regularity so often associated with it.

The introductory bars given to the piano immediately capture the Serbian ethnic flavor. All three stanzas are exactly alike musically, but in the last the vocal part continues over what had been a solo piano interlude after the first two stanzas. This is a charming example of one of Brahms's many "composed folk songs."

"Mein Mädel hat einen Rosenmund" ("My Maiden Has a Rosebud Mouth") is a genuine folk song to which Brahms added a gay, flamboyant accompaniment. There is no variation in the four strophically set stanzas save that supplied by the interpreter, with the single exception of the marvelous final chord at the very end (each of the other stanzas breaks off abruptly). The text is a catalog of the sweetheart's attributes—her rosy mouth, her red cheeks, her dark eyes, her heavenly grace. Quite carried away in his enthusiasm the lad sings two refrains, "O du! o du! o du! " and "du lalalalala, du lalalalala" for which no translations are necessary. The sure touch of the master is evident in the exuberant two-bar piano solo and one bar of silence with which each stanza ends. Instead of the measure rest, Brahms gives us a triumphant and unexpected chord to bring the song to a rousing close.

"In stille Nacht," also counted among the folk songs for which Brahms merely provided accompaniments, is another matter altogether. Its subtle beauty is really Brahms's creation, for only the first few bars of the melody are actually from a folk tune. Once again we have a highly complex rhythmic concept that flows seamlessly and effortlessly, masking its intricacies to all but the practiced ear. The overall rhythm is 3/2, three half notes to a bar. With no introductory prelude, the piano begins on the eighth note before the third half note. This note is held just long enough for it to overlap the next eighth note, providing emphasis without accent. Meanwhile the singer begins one eighth note later, on the main beat. This basic pattern, which alternates with a simpler chordal accompaniment, makes of the song an elegant and poignant duet.

The melody is serene and lovely, as befits a description of the "Still Night." At times the accompaniment flows gently around the melody's more sostenuto line; in the chordal measures it supports the melody unobtrusively. This is one of Brahms's most beautiful songs.

Of Brahms's interesting contributions to the vocal chamber-music literature, his two songs with viola obbligato (Opus 91) and the two sets of *Liebeslieder Waltzes* (Opuses 52 and 65), which are scored for a quartet of singers (soprano, alto, tenor, and bass) and piano four-hands, are the most successful. The viola songs are settings of religious texts, but the second, "Geistliches Wiegenlied," a description of Mary rocking the infant Jesus to sleep, sounds like a lovely but totally human lullaby. This same poem was set more dramatically by Hugo Wolf, as well as by Max Reger (1873–1916) and others.

The enormous popularity of the first set of *Liebeslieder*

Waltzes prompted Brahms to write a sequel. As so often happens, the second set does not quite measure up to the first, which epitomizes the spirit of old Vienna.

Despite his dour reputation, Brahms was no stranger to the waltz. His Opus 39 Waltzes for piano four-hands, later arranged by him for piano solo (Opus 39a) and then, in response to enormous demand, published in simplified form for less virtuosic pianists, proved him more than capable in this lighter style. In fact Brahms is so skilled, that despite the unrelenting 3/4 time of the *Liebeslieder Waltzes*, there is plenty of variety in the delicious songs, all of which, of course, deal with the trials, tribulations, and triumphs of love.

Hugo Wolf
(1860–1903)

Leaping dizzily from pinnacle to pinnacle in the saga of the German art song, it becomes all too easy to think in a stream of superlatives, or, worse, to doubt the monotonously high praise lavished on one composer after the next. When we remember that Brahms was twenty-three years younger than Schumann and Wolf twenty-seven years younger than Brahms, it becomes apparent that although many lesser talents produced interesting and even beautiful songs during this heyday of lieder writing, only a few major figures emerge, and often decades separate them from one another. Interestingly enough three major art song composers were born in a cluster—Wolf and Mahler in 1860 and Richard Strauss in 1864. We shall discuss Wolf first.

To music lovers not particularly interested in the art

song, the name Hugo Wolf summons only the haziest of recollections. Yes, there is the lovely *Italian Serenade* for string quartet, later orchestrated, and the less familiar symphonic poem called *Penthesilea*, but were all of Wolf's non-vocal works to disappear, the concert world would scarely notice. This is certainly not true in the confines of the art song, for Wolf's approximately 250 songs are a treasure trove of wit, charm, dramatic intensity, religious fervor, erotic passion, and lyric beauty.

Like Schumann, Wolf was passionately devoted to literature. The poems he chose to set were invariably of the highest quality, and he was meticulous about matters of prosody, allowing the natural cadences of the texts to dictate melodic rhythms. It was his pattern to become infused with the spirit of one poet at a time, producing long series of songs based on poems of Heine, Eichendorff, Eduard Mörike, and Goethe. After the Goethe songs which were published in 1890, reluctant to use texts that had been successfully set by Schubert, Schumann, or Brahms (although he had previously done so) and feeling that the best German poetry had been exhausted by his predecessors, he turned to two sets of translations, one from the Spanish and one from the Italian. The German poet Paul von Heyse was responsible for all the adaptations in the *Italienisches Liederbuch*; Emanuel Geibel was his collaborator in the *Spanisches Liederbuch*. A few contemporaneous songs to texts of Gottfried Keller and Robert Reinick indicate that his interest in German poetry had not completely expired (in his youth he had used texts by Lenau, Chamisso, Friedrich Hebbel, von Fallersleben, and others). His last songs were to three poems by the great Italian sculptor Michelangelo.

When these last poems appeared (1898), Wolf was only thirty-eight years old. Although he was to live another five years, severe emotional stress and resultant mental illness prohibited further creativity, leaving his second attempt at opera, *Manuel Venegas*, unfinished. His only completed opera, *Der Corregidor*, is more successful in its brief, songlike vignettes than in its attempts to sustain dramatic interest, and is rarely performed.

Wolf's songs are enormously varied. Their emotional range includes the tragic severity of the religious songs based on Calvary, the tender devotional warmth of his portrayals of the Holy Family, the childlike whimsy of the fairy-tale songs, the bleak despair of unrequited love, the exquisite fulfillment of shared passion, the irony of the cynical, the innocence of the young—in short the sum of the human experience. Not even Schubert surpasses this all-encompassing expression of the inner life of man.

In general, except for the folk-song-inspired settings, Wolf avoids strophic form. His extreme sensitivity to each nuance of the words usually precludes exact repetition of the music. Instead we often have an almost symphonic development in the piano parts, whereby one or more themes—inspired of course by the words—are varied and developed, while the voice declaims in a free rhapsodic style. This makes the piano parts full, complex, and quite difficult to play. Sometimes, especially in the *Italienisches Lieder*, Wolf weaves the piano and vocal parts contrapuntally; occasionally, in complete contrast, the piano parts are spare and minimal.

Along with the obvious influences of Schubert and Schumann, Wolf's songs show the impact of the musical eminence of Richard Wagner. It was largely Wagner who moved so much of the musical development in opera from the vocal parts to the orchestra; it was also Wagner who stretched the whole diatonic tonic-dominant system of Western music to its limits with his endless chromaticism. Late nineteenth-century composers either loved or hated, accepted or rejected, Wagner—none could ignore him. Wolf's songs can be either simply diatonic or dissonant and chromatic, depending on the mood he was trying to create. Some of his songs are well within the nineteenth-century Romantic zeitgeist; others point directly to twentieth-century atonal and twelve-tonal developments.

We shall discuss the following representative songs: from the Mörike collection "Begegnung," "Um Mitternacht," "Das verlassene Mägdlein," "Elfenlied," and "Seufzer"; from the Spanish lieder book, "Die ihr schwebet" and "Geh' Geliebter, geh' jetzt"; from the Italian songbook, "Wir haben beide lange Zeit geschwiegen," "Wie lange schon," and "Mein Liebster singt." Very little time separates these three great collections, for the majority of Wolf's most important songs were composed in a few frenzied spurts of inspiration in the years 1888, 1889, 1890, and 1891. These include all the Mörike, Goethe, and Spanish songs, a ten-song set based on Eichendorff's poems, and book I of the *Italienisches Liederbuch.* After a hiatus of five years, Wolf picked up where he had left off to compose book II of the Italian songs, with no discernible change in style. Differences among these songs are due therefore not to any process of maturation in the composer, but to his total susceptibility to the demands of the poetry.

"Begegnung" ("The Meeting") describes two radiant but slightly embarrassed young lovers meeting the morning after. The first lines of the poem tell us that a storm has raged all night, and the piano's opening figure suggests the blustery winds and buffeting rains. When the voice enters, it follows the contours of the piano figure, rising ominously in a minor-scale fragment. A switch to the major modality prepares the scene for the young girl's appearance, and when she is introduced, the accompaniment becomes lighter and less threatening without losing its breathless, rushing quality. The young man appears after another key change and his own introductory piano interlude. When they see each other, the original storm figure returns in the accompaniment, obviously now the storm of their passion. As the maiden whisks past, leaving the youth dreaming of last night's kisses, the gentler accompanying figure returns, continuing after the words have finished in a nine-bar piano postlude which ends wispily, as though borne away on the winds. If it were not for some strong dissonances, this charming song would be quite Schubertian.

"Um Mitternacht" ("At Midnight") is a second example of a Wolf song with a continuously flowing piano accompaniment. Its 12/8 rhythm creates a subdued rocking effect beautifully suited to the words which describe the endless cycle of night into day, day into night. The waters seem unaware of the perfect balance of time, for they rush along singing, not keeping the silence of the night. For the first eleven bars of each of the two almost strophically treated stanzas, the accompaniment is kept to a low-pitched murmur with no profile of its own. The melody is based on the minor scale and its intervals are narrow. In the second half of each stanza, where the waves are described, the melodic intervals become wide and unusual, beginning with a rising seventh and featuring a dizzying fall under "Mutter, der Nacht." Here the accompaniment has ringing long notes at the beginning and middle of each measure, accentuating the rocking motion. The outstanding feature of the song is its highly original harmonic flavor, above all the pervasive use of minor seconds and major sevenths, which sound strange and awesome.

The brief, poignant picture of "Das verlassene Mägdlein" ("The Forsaken Maiden") uses a completely different style to equally powerful effect. Here the piano part is spare and simple, the mood static, the rhythm hypnotically repetitious. The poem is terse enough to quote in full:

When the stars are still shining, I must rise and make the fire,
I get out of my bed long before daybreak.
Often I sit and stare at the gaily shining sparks;
My heart is heavy with care, filled with grief.

Ah, then it comes to me, thou faithless youth,
That I did dream of you in the night.
Tears after tears fall from my eyes;
The day has come at last—would that it were ended!

Sad little minor thirds open the four-bar piano introduction. The voice enters quietly on a high E (original key), only to fall wearily in the next measure. Most of the principal melody has a downward curve, ending an octave below its starting point. The middle section (the song is in ABA form) begins with a little more motion as the girl describes the fire's sparks, but her heart is too heavy to be lifted. One long piano interlude interrupts the B section, another separates it from the da capo, and a third ends the song. The harmonies are exquisite, featuring the augmented chords so dear to the hearts of such French song composers as Duparc, Chausson, Fauré, and Debussy.

With "Elfenlied" ("Elf's Song") we reach an example of Wolf's romantic fairy-tale songs, inspired in part by similar settings by Karl Loewe. "Nixe Binsefuss" and "Lied vom Winde" are also in this fey, whimsical style.

The song opens with voice and piano boldly ascending the tonic scale in unison, and then falling an octave. The words, "Eleven o'clock," the watchman cries, "hear me," match the music's sense of anticipation. Suddenly the dynamic level falls to pianissimo as we meet the wee elf who, awakened and startled by the watchman's loud cry, rubs his eyes and totters around quite drunk with sleep. The elf's clumsy dance is delightfully portrayed in the music, first by teetering octaves in the accompaniment and then by staccato notes in the piano's upper registers. At the end of the song the elf bumps his head on a stone. The singer intones "Poor elf" on rocking octaves and asks "have you had enough? Cuckoo! Cuckoo!" All the "cuckoos" are charmingly imitative, as are the piano's chords and skittery sixteenth notes.

"Seufzer" ("A Sigh") exemplifies the opposite extreme of Wolf's many-faceted nature. It is a stark, uncompromising, religious work in which the poet laments his inability to keep and cherish the love of Christ. Dissonances abound in the accompaniment, the opening chords stressing the clash between the tonic note and the note one-half step beneath it (a major seventh up). The heavy 4/4 rhythm, with its dynamic rise to the second beat and falling away on the fourth, makes of almost every measure an audible sigh. The melody sighs too, as it falls on the words, "hegen," "pflegen," "Herzen," and "Höllenschmerzen." No solace is offered in the brief song which ends with grief-laden chords.

Of the forty-four songs in the *Spanisches Liederbuch*, ten are to religious texts and thirty-four to secular—mostly love—poems. "Die ihr schwebet um diese Palmen" ("Among the Floating Palms"), which deals with the Holy Family, is one of the warmest and most lyric of the religious songs. Brahms also set this poem, in which Mary tends the sleeping infant Jesus. She asks the angels to silence the breezes for "es schlummert mein Kind" ("my babe is asleep"), the refrain of the song.

Brahms's setting is a tender, human lullaby. Wolf's keeps the song on a celestial plane, giving to the piano a shimmering figure which evokes angels' wings and an ethereal atmosphere. The piano's left hand supports much of the vocal line while the right hand supplies tremolo harmonies.

This same figure well serves the lines dealing with the wind rushing through the palms, but seems less suited to the verse in which Mary says that the heaven-born infant knows earthly sorrows. Fortunately the words soon return to the idea of the wind in the palms. A change from the major to the minor mode, harsh accents, and many high notes in the vocal part distinguish the words "Cold blows the wind and the Mother is weeping," but a final statement of the refrain brings back the major modality and tranquillity. Despite continuous use of the one accompanying motif, the song is through-composed with no real repeats.

The last song in the Spanish lieder book, "Geh' Geliebter, geh' jetz," is one of the most exquisite love songs ever written. In a refrain heard four times, at the beginning of each of the three stanzas and as an epilogue, the woman sings to her lover:

> Geh', Geliebter, geh' jetzt!
> Sieh, der Morgen dämmert.
>
> Go, beloved, go now!
> See, the morn is dawning.

The music for the refrain is gentle and limpid, speaking of tenderness and the languor of spent passion. The two lines of verse are surrounded by a melting accompaniment, composed of descending triplet octaves in the right hand and pulsating chords in the left. The opening two bars build to a traditional dominant-seventh chord, but in a most unusual and subtle way. The beguiling vocal line is woven into the highly chromatic accompanying octaves as though in an impressionistic haze, and the entire section is mesmerizing in its dreamlike beauty.

The first and second sections between the refrains are quiet, but the third is agitated and intense. The motifs and figurations of the accompaniment do not change from section to section; instead they develop harmonically and expressively. In the first stanza the vocal line is largely declamatory, with one note repeated for many syllables, very much in the style of Fauré or Debussy. The melodic line in the second stanza is more expressive, as the lovers lament their need to part. The last section is full of passionate urgency as she tells him

> Flieh denn aus meinen Armen!
> denn versäumest du die Zeit
>
> Flee then from my arms
> lest you forget the time.

for she knows great grief will come to them if their love is discovered. In a hushed, strangely chromatic phrase she says that although they may suffer purgatory's fires, hope for their love gives them the glories of heaven. Under these last words, "in Strahlen lässt des Himmels Glorie sehn," the accompanying octaves rise triumphantly in a tremendous crescendo to a climactic fortissimo. The song ends quietly with a repeat of the refrain.

The Italian songbook consists of forty-six one-sided conversations between lovers—we hear either his side or hers. Since Wolf was no conscientious objector in the war between the sexes, the men are usually tender or passionate and the women are often scornful, cynical, angry, or terribly unhappy. Many of the songs are deliciously comic—one tells of the handsome Toni who is starving himself to death over unrequited love by eating a sausage and seven loaves for every molar after every meal—but many are quite poignant. Although one occasionally hears Hispanic rhythms and guitarlike chords in the Spanish songs, nothing really marks Wolf's settings of the *Italienisches Liederbuch* as Italian.

"Wie lange schon" ("How Long It's Been") is one of the comic vignettes. A young lady says that she has always wanted a musician for a lover and now she has one who is all pink and white, "spielt die Violine." The music is mock-serious until the wonderful epilogue in which the piano imitates a fiddler massacring his instrument.

In "Mein Liebster singt" ("My Lover Sings"), a heartbroken young girl weeps while her lover serenades her. Since she shares a bed with her mother she can't join her lover, can't even let him know she hears his song. The accompaniment is entirely given over to the serenade, with its simple melody and strummed chords. The young Romeo plays his song over and over in sweet homage. The melodic line is much more static, reflecting the girl's inability to move. The falling vocal line under "Blut sind die Tränen die mir nicht versiegen" ("My tears flow like blood and do not dry") ends with a strange, sad cadence. Her anguish is very real.

As our last example of Wolf's expressive range we offer "Wie haben beide lange Zeit geschwiegen" ("In Silence Each the Other Passed"), a song of reconciliation after a lovers' quarrel. At first the ominous sound of the piano's descending unisons and the repeated notes of the singer's slowly rising declamatory line describe the lovers' heavy sorrow over their rupture. Suddenly we hear a warm major chord at "die Engel" ("the angels"), for peace and happiness have been restored by God's angel. From this moment on the piano has its own little song to play, its melodic line interwoven in beautiful counterpart to the vocal part. Only one lover is speaking, but it's a duet that we hear. The piano plays its brief song three times, twice while the words still flow and once as an epilogue. At the second hearing its chords are arpeggiated to suggest angels' harps. The song is an elegiac paean to true love.

Gustav Mahler and Richard Strauss

(1860–1911)   (1864–1949)

Of the three contemporaries, Wolf, Mahler, and Strauss, only Wolf died at the dawn of the twentieth century. Mahler lived until 1911 and Strauss survived the two world wars. Since Wolf's significant output consists only of art songs, it is in this genre alone that we can compare these composers. Strange to tell, Wolf's most advanced songs seem more contemporary than Strauss's last works, although the latter were written half a century later. This is due partly to Wolf's extraordinary harmonic originality and partly to the fact that Strauss's most adventurous experimentation was done before he turned forty, when Wolf was still alive and composing. Furthermore Strauss's most avant-garde ideas appear in his symphonic poems; in his songs he is the last great Romantic.

Strauss and Mahler share a passion for large orchestral works. Together they bring to a close the nineteenth-century Romantic symphonic era—almost exclusively a German phenomenon, if one is willing to place the peripatetic Franz Liszt within its confines. Despite the genius of Hector Berlioz and a handful of ethnically oriented composers, the overwhelming dominance of the combined symphonic works of Haydn, Mozart, Beethoven, Schubert, Schumann, Brahms, Mendelssohn, Bruckner, Mahler, and Strauss brooks no competition. To cap the list one must add Wagner, in whose works operatic orchestral writing was metamorphosed.

Both Strauss and Mahler enlarged the scope of orchestral music, feeling that the symphony orchestra could be used to describe external events and to express subtle emotional developments. In this they were disciples of Wagner and Liszt. For Mahler this implied the combination of art song with symphony: of his nine completed symphonies four include voice; of his six major song cycles four have orchestral accompaniments (of course there are piano-voice versions of these cycles). Strauss, veering off in a different direction, prodded the Lisztian symphonic tone poem to ever more explicit programs. *Don Juan, Till Eulenspiegels lustige Streiche, Also sprach Zarathustra, Don Quixote,* and *Ein Heldenleben,* all composed between 1888 and 1898, are highly original, marvelously orchestrated examples of his work in this genre. Strauss also wrote fifteen songs for voice and orchestra, but these are not focal works.

In the symphonic tone poems of Strauss and the symphonic song cycles of Mahler the orchestra takes on new color and luster. Often the French horn or oboe carries the tune instead of the strings; often one particular instrument—the viola or the oboe in many cases—represents one specific character (Berlioz anticipates this device in *Symphonie Fantastique* and *Harold in Italy).* Mahler is fond of bells, exotic percussion, and Oriental melodic undulations. Both are masters of harmonic polyphony, whereby individual melodic strands are interwoven contrapuntally within the context of the larger body of instruments. All these effects make the piano renditions of Mahler's orchestrally conceived cycles very pallid in comparison to the originals, although some songs work better than others.

Mahler's important songs are found in the following groupings: *Lieder und Gesänge aus der Jugendzeit* (1882), which consists of two songs with texts by Richard Leander, one traditional text, two by Nikolaus Lenau, and nine poems from an anthology of traditional German folk verse called *Des Knaben Wunderhorn; Lieder eines fahrenden Gesellen*

(1883), for which the composer wrote his own texts (the four songs describe his heartbreak over unrequited love); another large group of selections from *Des Knaben Wunderhorn* (1888); five separate songs to poems by Friedrich Rückert (1902), and the pathos-filled *Kindertotenlieder (Songs on the Death of Children)* for which Rückert also supplied the texts (1902). Of these only *Lieder und Gesänge aus der Jugendzeit (Youthful Songs and Airs)* and the five Rückert songs were originally conceived for voice and piano, although all are available with piano accompaniments. The last great cycle, *Das Lied von der Erde* (1908) is composed for orchestra, contralto, and tenor.

In a sense Mahler's songs are inseparable from his symphonies. The First Symphony uses material from the song cycle *Lieder eines fahrenden Gesellen* but no voices; the second incorporates the witty song "Des Antonius von Padua Fischpredigt" and other material from *Des Knaben Wunderhorn;* the third, scored like the second for orchestra, solo voices, and chorus, also contains themes from a *Knaben Wunderhorn* song, as does the fourth, which is scored for small orchestra and soprano.

Strauss's 125 songs form more of a separate entity. He is one of the few successful songwriters who also excelled in opera—*Salome, Elektra, Der Rosenkavalier,* and *Ariadne auf Naxos* are all valued staples of opera houses everywhere. His earliest songs are among his best; he ceased composing songs in 1929. His most popular operas are also fairly early, the post–World War I efforts now largely ignored. In fact his last important composition, the incidental music to *Le Bourgeois Gentilhomme,* was written in 1918, although he continued to compose steadily until 1948, the year before his death.

Limiting our study to works originally composed for voice and piano, we shall discuss the following songs: "Ich ging mit Lust durch einen grünen Wald" and "Aus! Aus!"

from Mahler's *Lieder und Gesange aus der Jugendzeit;*
"Zeitlose" (Opus 10 No. 7), "Ständchen" (Opus 17 No. 2),
"Wie sollten wir geheim sie halten" (Opus 19 No. 4), "Mein
Herz ist stumm" (Opus 19 No. 6), and "Heimliche Auffor-
derung" (Opus 27 No. 3) by Strauss.

"Ich ging mit Lust durch einen grünen Wald" ("I Went
with Joy Through a Green Wood") is a perfect example of the
lighthearted side of Mahler's nature. The text describes the
woods alive with birds gaily singing. When Madame Nightingale announces evening, the lovers meet and embrace. The
ominous conclusion of the poem, "You sleep-charmed maid-
en,/ Take care, take care!/ Where is your lover now?" is not
reflected in the music, which ends as it began, with birdlike
turns in the open key of C major (for low voice).

Much of the melodic line is based on tonic or dominant
chords. Bird sounds are imitated by grace notes, ornamental
turns, and beautifully undulating, slightly Oriental sixteenth-note passages in the accompaniment. One can easily
imagine a Mahlerian orchestration with bells and tambourines. Since this is what we might call a composed folk song,
rather than eschew strophic form, Mahler combines it with
da capo structure, giving us AABA. Despite the basic harmonic simplicity there are subtle coloristic touches, such as
the combined D major–A minor sound (this could be described as a D 7–9) under "grünen *Wald*" and in comparable
places in the other A sections.

The subject of "Aus! Aus!" is the eternal conflict between the young man who enthusiastically rushes off to war
and the despondent maiden he leaves behind. The two world
wars have effectively soured this long tradition of jaunty little
soldier songs, especially for Germans and Austrians of Jewish extraction such as Mahler. Fortunately Mahler was not
forced to face the ugliness of twentieth-century warfare, and
this song is gay and hearty.

In the tradition of the Brahms duet folk songs, "Aus! Aus!" is a dialogue interpreted by one singer. First we have the blustering soldier-to-be and then his sad sweetheart. The music leaves no doubt as to who's who, for the soldier has manly, straightforward melodies featuring a strong dotted rhythm, and accompaniments replete with drum-roll effects. Only once is he allowed to be a little more tender as he urges her to "Drink a glass of wine . . . and wipe your tears away." Whenever she speaks, there is a plaintive quality to the music and the drum rolls cease. The most significantly Mahlerian music in the song occurs when she sings "Ich will in's Kloster geh'n" ("I will go to a convent"), for over an unchanging open F chord (for low voice), the melody descends chromatically, with Oriental undulations on the way down. The piano's right hand follows the melodic line, harmonizing it in thirds. Of course her tears get her nowhere and he rushes off as fast as he can (there is an accelerando at the end).

Neither of these songs exposes the darker side of Mahler's emotional range, the intense pathos of *Kindertotenlieder,* or the eloquent melancholy of *Lieder eines fahrenden Gesellen,* for instance. Nor can they show his orchestral mastery, his imaginative scoring, the fine balance he achieves between solo voice and full orchestra. Fortunately records of his works by many fine interpreters are easily available.

Opera lovers who know Strauss's *Salome* and *Elektra* are aware of a strong morbid streak in this composer. "Zeitlose" ("The Saffron"), a tiny gem of a song based on a text by Hermann von Gilm, obviously appealed to that aspect of Strauss's psyche, for it describes a lonely saffron in a freshly mown meadow, from whose pure cup streams a red poison. "The last flower, the last love/ Are both beautiful, yet deadly," concludes the poem.

Strauss sets the words with great economy. The first

eight bars, which cover the neutral descriptive lines of verse, are in major, but at the words "Doch es ist Gift" ("Yet it is poison"), dark minor sounds predominate. The melody for these four words is chromatic and falling. The strongest sound is reserved for the syllable "töd" of the word "tödlich" ("deadly"), where the voice has a suspension C sharp over a G minor (tonic) chord.

There are almost as many "Ständchens" ("Serenades") as there are lieder composers. Strauss's differs from most in its quicksilver accompaniment, which must be played very softly so as to "awake no one from his slumber." This accompaniment is the brook that "hardly murmurs," the leaf that "scarcely flutters," her feet as she flies to him "with steps as gentle as those of elves." Since the accompaniment is often in high registers of the piano, it weaves its arabesques around the melodic line. The voice begins with a rising octave interval for the words "Mach auf, mach auf," expressing the impatience with which he awaits his loved one.

The poem, by A. F. von Schack, is in three six-line stanzas. The first two stanzas, which describe the scene and her flight to him, are treated strophically by Strauss. When she has finally arrived the music becomes dreamier, less fleet. The accompanying figure moves to the bass of the piano and the melodic line has longer notes with rests interrupting the flow. When the words say that the nightingale will dream of their kisses, the accompaniment—for the first time in the song—ceases its sixteenth-note figure in favor of an expressive little melodic interlude. This happens again three bars later, but the rustling figure returns for the last few words. The piano's epilogue combines melody and accompanying figure for a charming end to this delightful song, which makes its effect entirely within the range of traditional tonic-dominant harmony.

"Wie sollten wir geheim sie halten?" ("How Can We Keep Secret?") is another blissful poem by A. F. von Schack. Its central thought is expressed in the two lines "Wenn zwei in Liebe sich gefunden / Geht Jubel hin durch die Natur" ("When two in love have found each other / The joy spreads through nature"). Strauss's setting is ecstatic. Its soaring melodic line rises exultantly over shimmering accompanying chords, which remain harmonically static for several measures at a time. Because of this slow harmonic motion each modulation becomes an expressive focal point. One especially beautiful example is the change from C sharp minor to C sharp major under the sustained and repeated G sharp at the words *"Natur in längern"* (analyzed in the high voice key of A major). The celestial aura imparted by the high tessitura of the repeated chords yields to a warmer, more sensuous sound at "Selbst aus der Eiche . . ." A lovely progression leads to a triumphant C major chord and melodic triad at the climactic fortissimo at "Jugendlust" ("youthful joy"). The song ends with a solid dominant-tonic cadence in the vocal part and four additional measures of tonic chords for a piano postlude, as though Strauss is reaffirming his faith in the diatonic system of his predecessors.

"Mein Herz ist stumm" ("My Heart Is Silent"), yet another setting of a poem by Schack, has a bleak beginning and end. Strauss portrays the silent, cold heart, benumbed by winter's ice, with stark minor chords. Under the word "kalt" ("cold") there is a bitter dissonance. As the song progresses the heart begins to thaw, remembering green forests, blossoming meadows, murmuring brooks. For these more pleasant thoughts Strauss switches to the major mode, giving to the accompaniment gently rocking triplets and flowing sixteenth notes. Nevertheless the key line is "Doch das alternde Herz wird jung nicht mehr" ("Yet the aging heart will never more be young"), and the bleak mood of the opening must return. The most interesting feature of the song is the series of rapid modulations leading to this crucial line of verse from the words "ohr mir matt." This is a miniature version of the endlessly modulating passages one often finds in Strauss's tone poems.

With "Heimliche Aufforderung" ("The Secret Invitation," text by John Henry Mackay), we return to the exuberant joy of shared passion. Two lovers have arranged a tryst in the garden after the feast. Rhapsodically he tells her to eat, drink, and be merry before she slips away to meet him. The last lines, are "Oh, come you wondrous/ Longed-for night!"

The piano opens with cascades of notes—fourteen sixteenth notes to each bar. This "extra" note in each half measure immediately creates the desired aura of wild impetuosity. The rising melodic line is as assertive as a bugle call, as he confidently summons his inamorata. Every once in a while the rushing accompanying figure breaks off abruptly in favor of woodwind-like chords. At "Doch hast du das Mahl genossen" ("After you have savored the meal") all activity ceases as the piano plays quiet repeated notes and the voice declaims on two alternating pitches. Additional contrasting sections of calm and excitement and a tranquil epilogue complete the song.

When this song was written (1893–94) Strauss had not as yet composed any of his famous operas (only *Guntram,* his first, had been completed); nevertheless the harmonies in the song will seem familiar to those acquainted with *Der Rosenkavalier* and *Ariadne auf Naxos,* as will the stylistic device of periods of harmonic stasis alternating with periods of quicksilver modulations. In mood and in scope the song is quite operatic, giving us more than a glimpse of Strauss, the opera-composer.

Arnold Schoenberg and Alban Berg

(1874–1951)   (1885–1935)

Even among dedicated music lovers, the name Arnold
Schoenberg has been known to make strong men blanch,
conjuring as it does the essence of intellectuality, humorless
dogma, and craggy dissonance. Many regard his works as
music to be analyzed, but not enjoyed. There is no doubt that
much of Schoenberg's work is indeed difficult, even forbidding, and yet, do the lines

> If I do not touch your body today
> The thread of my soul will break
> Like an overstretched bow-string

seem likely to appeal to a dried-up intellectual? or the words

> . . . thank God and be quiet
> That you are still alive and kissing

to a humorless pedant? Would a bloodless theoretician
choose this description of Chopin's music

> Crimson chords of fierce desire
> Splatter despair's white-icy dream
> . . . .
> Hot exultant, sweetly longing
> Melancholy nightwood waltz

as a text for his own composition? These lines occur in
Schoenberg's Opus 15, *Das Buch der hängenden Gärten,*
Opus 48 No. 1, "Sommermüd," and Opus 21, *Pierrot-Lu-*

naire, respectively. Far from being exceptions, they are typical of the verses that inspired his romantic Viennese soul.

Schoenberg comes at the end of the long tradition of Austro-German Romanticism. He is the heir of Brahms, Wagner, Strauss, and, above all, Mahler. His earliest works, which include several charming, lightweight, trivial cabaret songs, are logical extensions of the developments of the previous generation. His first published compositions (Opuses 1 –3, 1898–1900), a dozen songs culled from a larger number of youthful efforts in this genre, are still based on conventional tonality. The first of the group, "Dank" (Opus 1 No. 1), or "Thanks," is typical of the overall style—an ecstatic vocal line supported by an impassioned, virtuosic piano accompaniment. The influence of Brahms is seen in the thick texture and complex passage work of the piano part, the influence of Wagner in the highly chromatic harmonies. A traditional dominant-tonic final cadence leaves no doubt as to tonal center. The music is extremely expressive, but in a feverish, supercharged way. This convulsive depiction of inner emotions has been labeled expressionism in art and music; in art it implies free distortion of form and color to convey inner sensations or emotions, particularly emotions associated with violence or morbidity. It is a particularly German phenomenon.

In Opus 2 several of Schoenberg's mature characteristics can already be heard. Perhaps the most important of his stylistic trademarks, since it differentiates his music most clearly from that of Wagner, Strauss, and even Mahler, is the rigid avoidance of melodies derived from the triad. Highly chromatic though Wagner, Strauss, and Mahler were, they often featured melodic triads—a time-honored custom—and Schoenberg's rejection of this basic 1–3–5 sequence is a departure of the utmost significance. All his future theoretical developments were to stress the importance of avoiding the triad—major or minor—harmonically as well as melodically; in these early songs he still accepted the triad harmonically, as final consonance.

The four songs of Opus 2 are full of harmonic innovations, some of which were simultaneously being developed by Debussy and Scriabin. The vague augmented chords, whole-tone scale fragments, and preponderance of notes foreign to the basic harmonies used by these composers served to weaken the whole system of key relationships, preparing in Schoenberg's case for a total break with tonality. To replace the usual emphasis on key relationships, chord progressions, and modulations, Schoenberg gives us an intricate polyphonic texture with much movement in the inner voices. There seems to be endless motivic variation with neither repetition nor sequential patterns—polyphony without imitation. Each moment, each phrase, each fragment is intensely expressive of the word being sung. Melody and accompaniment are in a constant state of flux.

The first song of Opus 2, "Erwartung" ("Expectation," not to be confused with his operatic monologue with the same title, Opus 17, 1909), has a strange surrealistic text by Richard Dehmel which describes a man standing silently:

> Her dark image gleams through the water,
> And he kisses her.

The second of the set, also by Dehmel (as is the third), is full of religious and erotic symbolism, a recurrent combination in Schoenberg's chosen texts. It is called "Jesus Bettelt" ("Jesus Begs"), and it is a strange version of the Mary Magdalen story:

> Give me your golden comb; every morning may it remind you
> To kiss my hair.

Only the fourth song of the opus, "Waldsonne" ("Forest

Sun"), with poem by Johannes Schlaf, has a lighthearted text and carefree music. The words "goldenen," "glänzen," "grüngolden" ("golden," "gleaming," and "green-gold") figure repeatedly in the text.

The six songs of Opus 3 (1898–1900), eight songs of Opus 6 (1905), two ballads of Opus 12 (1906–7), and two songs of Opus 14 (1907) are similar in style to those discussed above, but with *Das Buch der hängenden Gärten* (Opus 15, 1908), a new phase in Schoenberg's development is reached, for in this long cycle, based on fifteen Symbolist poems by Stefan George, Schoenberg abandons tonality completely.

To Schoenberg this step seemed inevitable, for perpetual modulation and extensive chromaticism had already subverted the tonic-dominant system. As a new expressive device, Schoenberg wanted to free dissonance, to make it the equal of consonance. To accomplish this he felt that the ear must be denied the familiar chord combinations, especially the triad. Furthermore no one note should be considered the tonal center, the note toward which all others gravitate. Harmonies should be used only for expressive, coloristic purposes, not as resting places or focal points, for if a particular consonance is heard as tonally central, all other chords, especially dissonances, are and must be subservient to it. Dissonances need not resolve—they must stand independent.

If there is no tonality, there can be no modulation, no moving from one tonal center to another. Linear writing, that is to say pure polyphony, must replace harmonic movement as an organizing principle. Every note must be significant, as none can be accepted as part of a preconceived harmonic or scale pattern. This must lead to very concise writing resulting in brief, terse compositions. The ideal vehicle for this revolutionary kind of music was of course the song cycle, for the words could provide structure, rhythmic organization, and an emotional framework. Thus it is no surprise that Schoenberg's first major atonal (a term Schoenberg never liked but which is currently used to indicate music without tonal center or "key") composition should be a song cycle, *Das Buch der hängenden Gärten*.

The fifteen poems by Stefan George on which this cycle is based are well suited to Schoenberg's nervous, fragmentary vocal lines and accompanying figures. They are highly emotional and often erotic, owing much of their exotic symbolism to works of French Symbolists Charles Baudelaire, Stéphane Mallarmé, and Paul Verlaine. The lines already cited from the eighth poem of the cycle, plus the following extract from the ninth, give an idea of the nature of the texts:

> [one kiss] is like one drop of rain spilled
> Upon a seared bleak desert,
> Which swallows it unslaked,
> . . . .
> And bursting with new fire.

Schoenberg's vocal lines for these texts often resemble pitched speech, a device he was to carry much further in *Pierrot-Lunaire* (see below). They are quite different from Debussy's declamatory lines, in which one note is often repeated for several syllables; indeed they are in constant motion and often feature extremely wide melodic leaps. Since each melodic fragment must express the word being sung, there is no audible repetition of vocal line or accompanying figure. None of the familiar traditional sounds—triads, cadences, leading tones, scales—beguile the ear, which must listen with intense concentration to the ever-evolving lines. The music does not lack expressivity—it is supercharged with emotions—but the expression is raw, untamed by traditional musical devices, untouched by conventional ideas of beauty. From the piano's single notes in the long introduction

to its harsh octaves and chords in the epilogue, nowhere is
there is hint of tonality in this remarkable thirty-minute
opus. Will it please every ear? No. Is it worth the effort it
takes to really hear it? Yes, indeed.

Schoenberg's next effort in the realm of vocal music was
his operatic monologue of 1907, *Erwartung* (*Expectation,*
Opus 17). The action in this psychological melodrama takes
place in the mind of its single character, who wanders
through the woods in search of her beloved. When she finally
finds him he is dead. The orchestral accompaniment is highly
dissonant. Once again polyphonic complexity replaces harmonic structure, and the expressivity is directly related to the
words.

Five years later (1912) Schoenberg published one of his
most fascinating works, *Pierrot-Lunaire* (Opus 21) which is
scored for speaker, flute (doubling on piccolo), clarinet
(doubling on bass clarinet), violin (doubling on viola), cello,
and piano. The outstanding feature of the twenty-one-song
cycle (or "thrice seven" as the Cabalistically oriented
Schoenberg put it, deliberately matching opus number to
number of poems) is the use of "Sprechgesang" or "speech
song" (sometimes called "Sprechstimme"), a cross between
spoken and vocalized sounds based on given intervals and
rhythms but with no fixed pitch. Occasionally a word or
phrase is spoken or sung normally, but the bulk of the vocal
line is in this intoned declamation which is actually closer to
song than speech. The combination of instruments varies
with the poems, number seven of part I ("The Sick Moon")
scored for solo flute and voice, others using from two to all
five instrumentalists.

The texts are German translations by O.E. Hartleben of
French Symbolist poems by Belgian-born Albert Giraud
(1860–1929). Schoenberg chose twenty-one of Giraud's fifty
poems concerning Pierrot-Lunaire, a tragicomic figure repre-

senting maladjusted, alienated, modern man, and arranged them in three groups of seven songs each. The poems are all in a complex rondeau form which allows the first line of the poem to reappear as the third line of the second stanza, and again as an addendum to the third stanza (ABCD/EFAB/ GHIJA).

In part I, Pierrot gets divinely drunk on moon wine and is caught in a maelstrom of erotic longing. The fifth song of this section which describes Chopin's music has already been quoted. The sixth, "Madonna," conveys religious hysteria ("In thy fleshless wasted hands / Thou holdest the corpse that was thy Son"), and the seventh, an eerie neurasthenic fantasy bordering on parody, bemoans the "stanchless, quenchless ache of love."

Part II finds Pierrot in the depths of the underworld where he experiences guilt and suffering. The first song, entitled "Night," has a mysterious, ominous feeling created by the use of low, brooding notes in the piano and a low vocal tessitura. The fourth song, which returns to religious hysteria, is virtually shrieked by the vocalist as she hurls the words like curses:

At the gruesome Eucharist . . .
He holds aloft to trembling souls
The holy crimson-oozing Host:
His ripped-out heart—in bloody fingers.

This is followed by "Gallows Ditty," which is spoken quickly like doggerel. The macabre mood continues through No. 6 ("Beheading"), yielding to a more dramatic aura for No. 7 ("The Crosses") which explains that "Poems are poets' holy crosses."

In part III the hero of this picaresque series of adventures finds "A happy ending so long yearned for" as his "bitter mood has turned to peace" (No. 7). Several of the songs in this last section are quite gay, especially No. 4 ("The Moon Fleck," in which Pierrot tries to rub out a spot of moonlight which has fallen on his jacket—a vaudeville-inspired metaphor for expiation of guilt), and No. 5 ("Serenade": "With grotesquely giant-sized bow / Pierrot draws cat squeals from his viola").

Like the songs of Opus 15, the music for *Pierrot-Lunaire* is fiercely expressionistic. Intoned declamation is a wonderful vehicle for a singer with powerful acting ability (the Nonesuch record starring Jan de Gaetani is remarkable), for in "Sprechgesang" raw emotion need never be sacrificed to beauty of line or sound. The use of five instrumentalists with flexibility enough to handle eight instruments allows great variety of sound combinations while still guaranteeing linear clarity. In all, the work is gripping on an emotional level as well as fascinating on an intellectual plane. It was Schoenberg's penultimate Expressionist work, followed by Four Songs with Orchestra (Opus 22) and a ten-year hiatus in his output.

During the decade from 1913 to 1923, Schoenberg was preoccupied with the problem of the structural organization of nonvocal music without recourse to tonality. Eventually he hit upon the solution of the twelve-tone row, whereby every one of the twelve tones into which the octave is subdivided must be heard once before any can be repeated. Furthermore within the row any suggestion of the triad, the leading tone or the V–I combination, must be avoided. The word "row" is a bit deceptive, for the notes need not be sounded one at a time—several may be played in combination provided that they do not form a consonance. The row should have a distinctive rhythmic pattern, as its serial combination will probably not be easily recognizable. The row can be inverted, played on various pitch levels, and otherwise manipulated throughout the piece. The last piece of Opus 23, five short pieces for piano, was the first to use this so-called serial technique.

Although all of Schoenberg's subsequent works, including the opera *Moses und Aron*, were affected by this new technique *(Von Heute auf Morgen*, Schoenberg's Opus 32, 1929, is the first twelve-tone opera), the three songs of Opus 48, written in 1932 but published much later, are Schoenberg's only strictly 12-tone songs. The use of the twelve-tone row does not appreciably affect Schoenberg's vocal style and these songs resemble his presprechstimme vocal works.

Schoenberg used declamation with orchestra in three later pieces: *Kol Nidrei* (1939), *Ode to Napoleon* (1943), and *A Survivor from Warsaw* (1947), but none has the power of *Pierrot-Lunaire.*

Two extremely talented composers, Anton von Webern (1883–1945) and Alban Berg (1885–1935), are Schoenberg's best-known disciples. Webern's contribution to vocal music consists only of two cantatas for soprano and orchestra, but Berg wrote several sets of songs including Five Songs for voice and orchestra based on picture-postcard texts by Peter Altenberg (Opus 4, 1912), Seven Early Songs (1905–8) and the Four Songs, Opus 2 (1908–9). He also composed many single songs, including "Schliesse mir die Augen beide" and "An Leukon," and a Canon for four voices (1930) based on a twelve-tone theme from Schoenberg's *Von heute auf Morgen.* His most important vocal works are his operas *Wozzeck* (1925) and *Lulu* (unfinished but produced posthumously).

Berg's romantic temperament made him somewhat lenient in his adherence to Schoenberg's specifications for serial technique. Major or minor triads sometimes creep into his tone rows and one senses a compromise between the new music and the old tonality. We have chosen to discuss the two versions of "Schliesse mir die Augen beide" ("Close My

Eyes") which Berg wrote in 1900 and 1925 respectively, since the differences between them tell much about his development while the similarities indicate his basic characteristics.

The text, written by Theodor Storm, is an anguished cry to the beloved. He wants her hands to close his eyes when he is gone "that my anguish and suffering may find peace at thy sweet touch." Berg's early setting is in the key of C major. Its romantic, flowing melody is closely supported by the accompaniment which has a rich harmonic texture with few discords. Melody and harmony join in a perfect V–I cadence at the end.

The second setting—not a revision, a completely new composition—is in serial technique. The melody begins with a twelve-tone row which is repeated with inner inversions (for example: the first statement of the row begins with an F natural and goes to the E natural one-half step below; in the third statement of the row the F goes to the E not quite an octave above) throughout the song. In all there are five statements of the row. The last note of the row, a B natural, usually occurs in the middle of a phrase, making it very difficult for the ear to hear the new beginning. This is deliberate, for, unlike themes used imitatively in eighteenth-century polyphony, the row is the technique, not the musical point.

The accompaniment begins with its own twelve-tone row, nine notes played sequentially and the last three as a chord. This row is not used consistently but does reappear after the fourth line of verse (midway in the song). The two rows do not resemble each other. At one crucial point in the song, under the word "leide" ("pain"), Berg allows the accompaniment to echo the voice's falling phrase, after which the piano continues with a fragment of the singer's row.

Despite the strange melodic intervals and uncompromising discords, the romantic nature of the song is not lost. The melody rises and falls expressively to match the words, and the accompaniment moves slowly or precipitously in sympathy with the meaning of the text. This is true of Berg's Four Songs, Opus 2, and indeed most of his output.

Hector Berlioz, Charles Gounod, César Franck, and Georges Bizet

In a way this study follows the format of the conventional song recital. Having warmed up with "early" songs, and having provided a fair sampling of the enormous body of German lieder, we are now ready to move on to the next most important segment of the art song literature, the French mélodie.

French music, along with French art and literature, dominated European culture in the Middle Ages. During the Renaissance, Italy took the lead in architecture and painting, but French King François I, who reigned from 1515 to 1547, imported hundreds of Italian artists and artisans to bring the fruits of the Renaissance to France. Over one hundred years later (1661–1715), the brilliance of the court of Louis XIV, the Sun King, assured French preeminence in arts and letters. Lully (1632–1687) was Louis XIV's favorite musician, and his operas were among the glories of the court.

François Couperin (1668–1733) and Jean Philippe Rameau (1683–1764), the next generation's leading French musicians, wrote with grace and wit, but did not possess the transcendental genius of their contemporaries, Bach (1685–1750) and Händel (1685–1759). Thus, early in the eighteenth-century, leadership in instrumental music and art song moved to Germany and Austria, while Italy retained her position as the principal land of opera, leaving France far behind musically for the better part of a century.

During this musically quiescent time, French genius focused on philosophical and political thought. Montesquieu, Voltaire, Rousseau, and others challenged the established order, and the Revolution of 1789 finally brought an end to the divine right of kings. Under Napoleon, who crowned himself emperor in 1804, one year after Berlioz was born, French culture rose like a phoenix from the ashes and Paris once again became the artistic capital of the world. In art song this brings us to Hector Berlioz (1803–1869), Charles Gounod (1818–1893), Belgian-born César Franck (1822–1890), and Georges Bizet (1838–1875). None of these composers created bodies of work comparable to the songs of their contemporaries Schumann or Brahms (Schubert was just a bit earlier), but all of them had an important influence on the far more interesting and original songwriters of the next generations—Chausson, Duparc, Fauré, Debussy, and Ravel—who will be discussed in following chapters.

Berlioz was the quintessential nineteenth-century French Romantic. His life was full of tempestuous *affaires de coeur* which found expression in his compositions. While far from the initiator of program music, he was the first to put the initimate details of his passion in symphonic form (*La Symphonie Fantastique*) and to insist that the audience follow the plot blow by blow.

Like most Romantics, Berlioz saw things in larger-than-life dimensions, scoring his orchestral works for ever greater forces and envisioning choruses of six hundred or more singers. This tendency toward hyperbole, while enhancing his brilliant innate flair for orchestration (he has been called the father of modern orchestration), makes him less than the ideal songwriter. The most stirring art songs are those which quickly establish a mood and then make a strong emotional statement. Sometimes the contrast between conflicting emotions gives a song its power, but rambling discursiveness, melodramatic effects, and operatic effusiveness do not usually add up to first-rate art songs, and Berlioz is often guilty of all the above excesses.

A perfect example is "Sur les lagunes," the third of the six *Nuits d'Eté* Berlioz composed from 1834 to 1841 to texts of Théophile Gautier. The poem, subtitled "Lament," is the simple plaint of a fisherman whose love has died, leaving him alone on the vast sea. The refrain is a heartbroken "Que mon sort est amer! / Ah! sans amour s'en aller sur la mer" ("How bitter is my fate / Ah! without love, to wander on the sea"). Berlioz's setting is quite long, although the text is fairly brief (three stanzas plus refrain). Gautier's lines are terse and understated: "Ma belle amie est morte, / Je pleurai toujours" ("My beautiful love is dead, / I shall cry forever"), which gives them the ring of honest emotion, but Berlioz stretches the lines with operatic devices such as long-held high notes, robbing them of their authenticity and sincerity. The piano is given melodramatic tremolos under "Ah! comme elle était belle" (this section sounds much better in the orchestrated version). The dotted rhythm to the words "Que mon sort est amer" the second and third times the refrain is heard is yet another artificial touch. The chief merit of the song is the effective close on C major when the song has been primarily in F minor (analyzed in low-voice key).

It is interesting to compare this Berlioz song with a setting of the same poem by Gabriel Fauré (Opus 4 No. 1, composed about 1865). Instead of the fanciful title, Fauré calls his version simply "The Fisherman's Song." The barest accompaniment establishes the rocking rhythm of the sea, and the words are set as naturally as possible, making the song a little gem.

Two of Berlioz's more effective songs, "La Captive" (text by Victor Hugo) and "Zaïde" (poem by Roger de Beauvoir) have in common an invigorating Spanish flavor. Once again the orchestrated versions are superior to the original piano accompaniments, for Berlioz captures the sounds of castanets and strummed guitars with his colorful use of instruments. "La Captive" is a song of many moods, as a young woman vacillates between happiness where she is (for she has many suitors!) and yearning for her native Spain: "Si je n'étais captive / J'aimerais ce pays" ("If I were not a captive / I would love this country"). "Zaïde" is consistently gay and exuberant as the protagonist sings "Ma ville, ma belle ville / C'est Grenade au frais jardin" ("My city, my beautiful city / Is Granada of the fresh garden").

Berlioz wrote only twenty-eight songs for solo voice and piano, of which eleven were orchestrated. A far more prolific composer in this medium was Charles Gounod who composed some 130 solo songs. As in the case of Berlioz, Gounod's output was highly variable. His most successful work is of course his opera *Faust*, which was produced in 1859, but none of his twelve other operas has achieved a lasting place in the repertoire. His religious music sounds sanctimonious and tedious to twentieth-century ears, and many of his songs seem equally banal. Nevertheless his best songs—"Medjé," "Venise," or "Quand tu chantes," for example—have much grace and charm.

Jules Barbier, one of the two librettists for Gounod's *Faust* (the other was Carré) provided the text for "Medjé" or "La Chanson Arabe." While Gounod's setting is not particularly exotic, one oft-repeated ornamental arabesque in the accompaniment does give a mildly Arabian flavor to the song. The poem has three stanzas (Gounod treats them strophically), each ending in the refrain "Medjé! Medjé! La voix de l'amour même / Devrait te désarmer! / Helás! Tu doute que je t'aime / Quand je meurs de t'aimer." With each stanza the words become more desperate as he cannot convince her of his love, although he is dying from this passion. Consequently in verse 2, "La voix de l'amour" ("The voice of love") is replaced by "Les pleurs de l'amour" ("The tears of love"), and in the final section we have "Le sang de l'amour" ("The blood of love"). In Gounod's setting the main portion of each stanza is in the minor mode, and the refrain is in the parallel major. A piano epilogue ends the song in the minor mode giving us ABABABA form. The song is quite touching in its naiveté.

César Franck is included in this survey not because of his songs—he wrote sixteen rather unimportant such compositions—but because of the enormous influence he exerted on the next generation of French composers. His habitual use of the ambiguous augmented chord—the equivalent of C, E, and G sharp on the piano which, since the intervals between the notes are equal, is analyzable as from the key of C, E (if the C is spelled as B sharp) or G sharp (then the C must be spelled B sharp and the E will be called D double sharp)— became the trademark of the French school, and led to Debussy's whole-tone scale (C, D, E, F sharp, G sharp, A sharp, C). His pupils included Duparc and Chausson, two of France's most important songwriters, and his influence spread throughout the younger generation.

Of the four composers treated in this chapter, Georges Bizet wrote the most enchanting songs. Oddly enough Bizet regarded his almost fifty songs as unimportant, and stopped composing in the genre around 1868. Fortunately many delightful songs appeared before he turned from the form.

Among the most stirring of Bizet's songs is the plaintive "Vous ne priez pas." In the poem (by Casimir Delavigne) a young woman sorrowfully accuses her faithless lover of forgetting his promise to pray for her: "Hélas! Hélas! J'écoute, et vous ne priez pas!" ("Alas! Alas! I listen, and you do not pray!"). The melody has many of the exotic 1 1/2-step intervals found in Hebraic and Moorish laments, and in fact sounds more Arabic than Gounod's "Chanson Arabe." Bizet is not afraid to use a strong dissonance under a key word (at "Je viens" he writes a D in the melody against a C sharp at the top of the accompaniment). He provides a beautiful chromatic effect under "je prierai pour toi" and a splendid modulation at the end of each verse, when he returns to the tonic (D minor for high voice) by way of an enharmonic change from A flat to G sharp in the melody. (An enharmonic change is one in which the pitch of a note remains constant, but its meaning changes because of a change in the underlying harmony. The change in meaning—from the first note of an A flat chord to the third note of an E chord, for instance—necessitates a change in the "spelling" or name of the note.) The song's only weakness is its strophic form, for the effects made seem too striking to bear immediate repetition in the second verse, and the unchanging accompanying figure becomes monotonous when heard over both verses.

An equally powerful song is "Adieux de l'hôtesse arabe" (1866), another example of Bizet's exotic writing. Since the music of the Spanish gypsies was influenced by Moorish melodies, it is not too surprising that the composer of *Carmen* should have exploited this spicy flavoring in his songs. The author of this sad farewell, sung by an Arab woman obviously in love with the European traveler who is about to leave her, is Victor Hugo. Hugo was the romantic versifier par excellence, and exotic settings had a strong appeal for him. The song abounds in Oriental 1 1/2-step intervals and melodic arabesques. In fact the long cadenza given to the singer at the end—an enormous arabesque—requires great facility and breath control.

In a different mood is the piquant "J'aime l'Amour," whose poem by Louis Gallet explains "Si l'amour parfume mon âme / Qu'importe la source . . . Que l'esclave soit brune ou blonde / Je cède au charme tour á tour / Je n'aime aucune femme au monde / J'aime l'amour!" ("If love perfumes my soul / What difference does the source make . . . Whether the slave is brunette or blonde / I yield to the charm of each in turn / I don't love any woman in the world / I love love!") This song has the jaunty effervescence and musical nonchalance of a music-hall number, foreshadowing similar repertoire from Poulenc, Satie, and others.

Bizet's charming "Berceuse" ("Lullaby") is based on a traditional French air. Its tender poem by Mme. Desbordes-Valmore is well-served by Bizet's unpretentious setting with its gently rocking 6/8 meter and simple harmonies.

"Chanson d'Avril" (text by Louis Bouillet) is a lovely song marred only by serious lapses in prosody. For example the second syllables of "lève" and "mouches," which should hardly be pronounced at all, both fall on downbeats, so that the singer is forced to say "lève" and "mouches." Nevertheless Bizet's use of countermelody in contrary motion to the main melodic line is so charming that the song deserves to be heard.

Gabriel Fauré

(1845–1925)

The two outstanding vocal works produced by the composers discussed in the previous chapter, Gounod's opera *Faust* and Bizet's opera *Carmen*, while certainly French in musical style, both include important non-French elements: *Faust* was of course inspired by Goethe's novel, and *Carmen* exploits the flavor of Spanish folklore and music. The next generation of French art song composers, Fauré, Duparc, Chausson, and Debussy, was much more intimately associated with the poetry of its own language, poetry that had reached a new pinnacle of beauty and power.

In 1857 Paris was startled by a major literary event, the publication of Charles Baudelaire's collection of poems *Les Fleurs du Mal* (*The Flowers of Evil*). This seminal work helped to create a new literary climate in France, for rejecting the "eloquent" overblown personal effusions of the Romantics, it aimed for an objective, detached portrayal of the most intimate, subjective emotions. Eventually known as Symbolism, this new style of poetry used analogy as its main figure of speech, expressing the universal correspondence among all the manifestations of nature and all the sensations and emotions of man.

Six years after the appearance of *Les Fleurs du Mal,* in 1863, the art world was transfigured by the exhibition known as "Salon des Refusés," the salon of painters rejected by the Royal Academy. Headed by Edouard Manet, these Young Turks ignored academic standards, insisting on their right to paint what they saw rather than what they were supposed to see and to paint it objectively, with no moral judgment or allegorical disguise. Manet's *Le Déjeuner sur l'Herbe,* for example, a "refused" painting depicting two fully dressed men picnicking on the grass with two women, one nude and one scantily dressed, scandalized the academy because of its outdoor setting, its matter-of-fact detachment, and its cold arrogance. From this first exhibit grew the Impressionist school, the world's sunniest, most colorful major artistic movement.

In Paris, poets such as Paul Verlaine, Stéphane Mallarmé, Charles Marie Leconte de Lisle, Théophile Gautier, and Armand Silvestre mingled with Impressionist painters and young musicians, each group adding to the heady mix of creative talents. From this cross-fertilization arose the quintessentially French music of Fauré, Chausson, Duparc, Debussy, and Ravel. The characteristics of this French style are elegance, understatement, and an emphasis on pure sound rather than on architechtonic structure or thematic development. Nowhere in the music of the typically French composer will one find the boisterous humor of a Beethoven scherzo, the intellectual strength of a Bach fugue, or the colossal pretensions of a Wagnerian *Ring*. Implicit in the music of Fauré and his compatriots is the assumption that the audience is civilized, able to absorb the ephemeral, willing to listen carefully enough to appreciate subtleties, and beyond the need for obvious melodrama.

Of the composers mentioned above, Gabriel Fauré produced the largest body of songs—ninety-seven to be exact. The first twenty of these songs (Opuses 1–8) were published in 1865 when the composer was just twenty years old, many of the group having been written several years earlier. Obviously his talent was precocious and prodigious.

Among the early songs there are several tentative, inconsequential efforts, but a surprising number are very fine indeed. Two of the loveliest are "Sérénade Toscane" and the famous "Après un Rêve," settings of Romain Bussine's translations of Tuscan poems. (Fauré's identification with Verlaine and other French Symbolists had not yet been solidified.) The melody for "Après un Rêve" is unusually lush and passionate for Fauré, so much so that string players have claimed it for their repertoires, and transcriptions for cello, viola, and violin are often heard.

The "Chanson du Pêcheur" ("Fisherman's Song") mentioned in connection with Berlioz's setting of the same text by

Théophile Gautier (page 122) is also part of this early group, as is the charming "Lydia," which contains a musical pun in its use of the Lydian mode (the F scale without the B flat).

"L'Absent" (Opus 5 No. 3, text by Victor Hugo) is characterized by a quiet dignity. In it Fauré makes use of the deliberately monotonous semi-intoned melodic line—eight syllables on only two notes for the words "Celui qui venait ne vient plus" ("He who came comes no longer")—which becomes the salient melodic stylistic device of this period. "Au Bord de l'Eau" ("At the Edge of the Water," Opus 8 No. 1, poem by René Sully Prudhomme) has some lovely modulations based on suspensions (the introduction of most of the notes of a new harmony while retaining one note from the old, then finally "resolving" the suspension by belatedly moving the held-over note to its proper position in the new chord).

After the publication of Opuses 1–8, there is a fifteen-year hiatus in Fauré's career as composer of art song, as other musical forms captured his attention. In 1880 he returned to the song form with Opus 18 Nos. 1–3, "Nell," "Le Voyageur," and "Automne," and from that year until 1892 wrote at least one major group of songs every year.

The three songs of Opus 21, "Rencontre," "Toujours," and "Adieu," constitute Fauré's first cycle (their collective title is *Poème d'un Jour*). The poems by Charles Grandmougin give a classic Aristotelian structure to the cycle, with a clear beginning, middle, and end. The irony of the third song depends on its following the first two, making performance as a unit mandatory. Gallic sentiment pervades the cycle—the melancholy of the protagonist before he meets her, his relief from his "persistent torment" now that they have met, and his hopes that she will "shine on his closed soul" ("Rencontre"), followed by a passionate outburst in which he cries that he could no more leave her than the "immense seas could dry up their vast tides" ("Toujours"), and then the dry little denouement, sung ever so sweetly, in which he explains that "Alas, the longest loves / Are short! And I say while leaving your charms / Without tears, / Practically at the moment of my vow / Adieu!" ("Mais Hélas! les plus longs amours / Sont courts! / Et je dis en quittant vos charmes / Sans larmes, / Presqu'au moment de mon aveu, / Adieu!").

Fauré's settings for this cycle are little masterpieces of psychological insight. The plaintive tenderness of the first song, with its shifting harmonies, its limited dynamic range, and its constantly flowing accompaniment, expresses the wistful, tentative nature of the poem. The second song is one unbroken outburst of indignation and passion. Although Fauré provides a drop to a piano to contrast with the overall forte dynamics, he insists that the furious pace continue unabated from start to finish. The final song is the surprise ending. After all the romantic storm and stress of "Toujours," it opens with a quaint, antique-sounding piano introduction. Neither the innocuous little tune nor the polite harmonies prepare the listener for the perfectly staged punch line—"Adieu!"

Among Fauré's best-known songs is "Clair de Lune" (Opus 46 No. 2). Composed in 1887, it is the first instance of Fauré's use of a text by Paul Verlaine, the poet whose works then inspired "Spleen" (Opus 51 No. 3), the *Cinq Mélodies* of Opus 58, the nine-song cycle *La Bonne Chanson* (Opus 61, 1891–92) and the song "Prison" (Opus 83 No. 1, 1900). Debussy also set "Clair de Lune"—in fact he wrote two different songs to the poem—and several of the other Verlaine poems chosen by Fauré ("Mandoline," "En Sourdine," "Green," and "Il pleure dans mon coeur" which is called "Spleen" by Fauré).

Fauré's setting begins with a long piano prelude which

is really an independent piece, with its own distinctive melody and harmonic structure. The most absorbing aspect of the song is the way in which the vocal line interacts with the piano part—often they seem almost to disregard one another, while at other times they are in close harmony. For long stretches the piano's melody seems more singable than the vocalist's! The poem is typically Symbolist, full of strange metaphors, farfetched juxtapositions, and words chosen more for their sensuous sound than for their explicit meaning: "Votre âme est un paysage choisi, / Que vont charmant masques et bergamasques" ("Your soul is a chosen landscape / Where charming masqueraders and dancers go").

By this time Fauré had developed his stylistic characteristic of avoiding the dominant chord or leading tone as the prelude to the final tonic chord. His resourcefulness in inventing new final cadences is astounding, as this and other songs demonstrate.

Many consider the peak of Fauré's songwriting to be his nine-song cycle *La Bonne Chanson.* Paul Verlaine wrote the ecstatic poems used in the cycle in a burst of happiness over his betrothal. There is a purity and innocence to the verses that give them a surprisingly nonerotic character. Although the fifth song ("J'ai presque peur") expresses the fear of losing such great happiness and the fourth ("J'allais par des chemins perfides") contrasts the poet's former gloomy existence to his newfound bliss, the overall effect of words and music is one of tranquil joy. The most unabashedly romantic song in the cycle is "La Lune Blanche Luit dans les Bois" (No. 3) which describes "l'heure exquise," the exquisite hour, the time for dreams, when "The white moon shines in the woods." The song's two passionate climaxes (under "O bien aimée" and after "Rêvons, c'est l'heure") are almost operatic in dramatic intensity, but—passion spent—the song ends in an aura of blessed calm.

A less familiar but equally beautiful cycle is *La Chanson d'Eve* (Opus 95, 1907–10), a ten-song work to texts by Belgian-born Charles van Lerberghe. This is Fauré's most ambitious cycle, surpassing in dimension and seriousness of purpose even *La Bonne Chanson* and *Le Jardin Clos* (Opus 106, 1915–18), his other major cycles. It is a retelling of the Genesis story, with Eve as the main character.

"Paradis," the first song in the cycle, has an exquisite opening. With utmost simplicity Fauré expresses the awesome wonder of Creation. The piano hesitantly intrudes on the silent void with a single note, the tonic (E); the singer then echoes this note while the piano moves to the dominant (B) for harmony. A dissonance (C in the piano against B in the voice) resolves to an A minor chord before the singer's return to the tonic note, which the piano then surrounds with a pristine C major chord. The words are "C'est le premier matin du monde" ("It is the first morning of the world").

The celestial nature of words and music continues through most of the cycle, although not all the songs are of the remarkable caliber of the first. The third, "Roses Ardentes," is an ecstatic affirmation of Eve's oneness with the universe. Fauré's setting is full of ardor which is expressed by a series of rising melodic lines. In the fourth song, "Comme Dieu Rayonne," we hear references to "church" music in the chord progressions. The text is a glowing tribute to the physical beauty of God, described in the full flower of radiant youth. The accompaniment of "Eau vivante" (No. 6) murmurs and bubbles like the running water which Eve praises. Number 8 ("Dans un parfum de roses blanches") has a sensual text far removed from the earlier Old Testament–inspired poems, resembling a pantheistic celebration of nature. The last two songs, "Crépuscule" ("Twilight") and "O Mort, Poussière d'Etoiles" ("Oh Death, Dust of the Stars") return to the dreamlike reverence of the opening, accepting—nay, embracing—man's mortality. The music is solemn but not anguished, reinforcing the celebration of life, of physical beauty, of nature, and finally of death expressed in the words.

Ernest Chausson and Henri Duparc
(1855–1899)   (1848–1933)

Chausson and Duparc are two composers who made important contributions to the art song repertoire despite the brevity of their creative years. Chausson, one of the few musicians of note to have begun the serious study of music as an adult (he entered the Paris Conservatory at the age of twenty-five) was killed in a freak bicycling accident in 1899; Duparc, another relative latecomer to music, fell victim to a strange mental collapse in 1885 which left him incapable of further creative work.

Duparc made a deep and lasting impression on the musical world with a meager handful of works; his reputation rests almost exclusively on his sixteen solo songs. Chausson's output is considerably larger, including the lovely *Poème* for violin and orchestra, several symphonic works, three operas, a unique piece of chamber music for violin, piano, and string quartet, two lush works for voice and orchestra, and over thirty solo songs.

Chausson's interest in song form continued throughout his professional career. His Opus 2 (1882) consists of seven songs, and his last published works (Opus 36 Nos. 1 and 2, 1898) are the songs "Cantique à l'Epouse" and "Dans la Forêt du Charme et de l'Enchantement." Since he was already twenty-seven when his first songs appeared, even in these early works one can hear the characteristics of his mature style: a gentle melancholia, a sweet simplicity, and a vague aura of ennui. This translates technically to fluid and frequent modulations, repetitious accompanying figures, overriding chromaticism, and a preference for vague augmented chords.

The best known songs from Opus 2 are the first and last, "Nanny" and "Le Colibri." Both have texts by Leconte de Lisle which summon nature as witness to and allegory for erotic love, but while "Nanny" expresses the despair of lost love, "Le Colibri" is all ecstatic fulfillment. In "Nanny" the listener immediately meets the above-mentioned Chausson trademark—an unvarying broken-chord pattern in the accompaniment (Fauré's songs are often set this way too). The mournful descending chromatic melodic line with which the song begins, so expressive of the melancholia of the words, returns three times, emphasizing the poem's mood of weariness and sorrow.

"Le Colibri" ("The Hummingbird") is the most sophisticated song of this early opus. Its 5/4 meter tends to catapult the music from one bar to the next, as though a sixth beat has been skipped. This evokes the bird in flight: "The green hummingbird . . . Like a bright beam, escapes into the air."

The four songs of Chausson's Opus 8 form a cycle, although one often hears the songs performed individually. The introduction to "Nocturne," the first, and the postlude to "Nos Souvenirs," the last, are closely related; all the poems are by Maurice Bouchor, and there is an emotional logic to the order in which the songs are presented, "Nocturne" describing young love, "Amour d'Antan" reminiscing on love's first flowering, "Printemps" lamenting the loss of love, and "Nos Souvenirs" looking back on love with the serenity brought by the passage of time. Of the four songs "Le Printemps" is the most extended and the most effective. Its anguished mood is conveyed by a chromatic melody, harmonized in thirds, that seems more descriptive of winter winds than of spring. In the frenzied section at the end of the song, the protagonist seems wild with grief. The song is very rich harmonically with long stretches of continuous modulation.

Chausson's next group of songs, Opus 13 Nos. 1–4, begins with a setting of a poem by Paul Verlaine, "Apaisement," which was included by Fauré in his cycle *La Bonne Chanson*, where it is called "La Lune Blanche Luit dans les Bois." Chausson's setting begins with an allusion to Mendelssohn's "Wedding March," a reference perhaps to Verlaine's having written the collection of twenty-one poems from which this text is culled to celebrate his forthcoming marriage. The song's enchanting atmosphere is created by exquisite chords on which the melody seems to float. For once there is scarcely any activity in the accompaniment and the singer even has some unaccompanied measures. The key word in the poem is "Rêvons" ("Let us dream"), and the hushed, ephemeral high notes of the ending do indeed project a dreamlike quality which effectively evokes "l'heure exquise" ("the exquisite hour").

It would be hard to imagine a musical setting more descriptive of its poem than "La Caravane" (Opus 14), one of Chausson's best-known songs. In it the piano's relentless quarter-note chords graphically depict mankind's endless, painful march across what poet Théophile Gautier describes as "The Sahara of the world." Chausson uses repetitious returns to the main harmony to suggest a treadmill—man marches but goes nowhere. There is a turbulent section expressing anger at man's cruel fate in which the melodic line rises feverishly while the accompanying chords rise and fall with almost maniacal intensity. An abrupt change of mood is precipitated by a stunning modulation to an unexpected major chord, at the word "voit" in the line "Et voici que l'on voit quelque chose de vert" ("And here one sees something green"), which brings acceptance and exaltation to the remainder of the song. Toward the end, organlike chords suggest religious solemnity; they are still marching, but the funeral march has become a dignified and even joyous processional.

Chausson's cycle *Serres Chaudes* (*Hothouses*, Opus 24), five songs to mystic, almost surrealistic, poems by Maurice Maeterlinck, is filled with vaguely ominous gloom. Nowhere in the words or music of the cycle is there solace or peace, much less pleasure or joy. Maeterlinck's symbolic use of the hothouse evokes an aura of stifling heat and forced, unnatural growth. The poems, full of strange morbid images, are in fairy-tale style, couching bizarre metaphors in the simplest terms. The music ranges from the wild passion of the first song to the world-weariness, apathy, languor, and pain of the others. The second, "Serre d'Ennui," is probably the most effective of the set, for Chausson's music beautifully expresses the enervated languor of the text. The melody begins with a pessimistic falling line; it rises only to fall again as the words describe "the weeping moonlight" ("le clair de lune qui pleure"). Constantly shifting harmonies create an overall chromaticism well-suited to the vague scene glimpsed through "Closed windows deep and green, / Covered with moon and glass." In this song the stylistic traits shared by Chausson, Fauré, and Duparc—ambiguous harmonies, free-floating progressions, chords chosen for their sounds rather than analytic "meaning"—are particularly evident.

The last Chausson song we shall discuss is his oft-heard "Les Heures" (Opus 27 No. 1, text by Camille Mauclair), a concise little masterpiece of structural unity. A tolling bell, the piano's right-hand figure, never ceases from the first measure to the last. The melody slowly pirouettes around this note while changing harmonies provide variety of sound. The poem's refrain "une à une" ("one by one") and deliberately repetitious rhyme-scheme describe the inexorable passage of time. Strong clashes between the tolling bell and the melodic line create musical tension while suggesting the bell's clangorous overtones. The song has a limited dynamic range, never rising above a mezzoforte, and ending in the merest whisper.

In the few examples of his work to have survived his compulsion to destroy what he had written, Duparc created a sensuous yet ethereal world, a world laden with mystery and yearning. While his close affinity to Fauré and Chausson is often in evidence, his songs are distinctive enough to set them apart and to assure them of their own niche in the repertoire.

Duparc's songs bear no opus numbers and their exact chronology is uncertain. Those that are dated seem to have been written between 1868 and 1871 and none was composed after 1884. Since almost every one is a masterpiece, no process of maturation or development can be detected from one to the other. Among the most unforgettable are "L'Invitation au Voyage," "Soupir," and "Lamento," each of which creates an atmosphere of vague longing and disembodied eroticism, and the less typically tempestuous "La Vague et la Cloche." In the former mood we must also mention the beautiful "Phydilé," with its ripe, languid sensuality, and "Extase," a quiet song of repose and fulfillment. In the stormier vein we find "Testament," in which the tempestuous piano part frequently clashes with the vocal line, suggesting anger and pain.

"L'Invitation au Voyage," based on a text by Charles Baudelaire, describes the allure of a grown-up version of never-never land, a magical place where the delights are highly sensual. The ethereal quality of the music makes one envision some unearthly, unattainable paradise, although Baudelaire seems to have had Holland in mind when he wrote the poem. The piano begins the song with one of Duparc's favorite harmonic progressions—a tonic minor chord to a II_7 chord with a lowered fifth (A, C, E to B, D sharp, F, A in the key of A minor, for low voice). These chords alternate until measures 8 and 9, where we have an unexpected modulation (minor II to major I) which sounds like the sun breaking through the haze. The glorious A major chord comes on the word "ensemble" ("together") in the lines "Mon enfant, ma soeur, / Songe à la douceur / D'aller là-bas vivre ensemble" ("My child, my sister, / Think of the sweetness / Of going to live there together"). The refrain, "Là, tout n'est qu'ordre et beauté, / Luxe, calme, et volupte" ("There, all is order and beauty, / Luxury, calm, and sensuality"), is intoned on a repeated A (tonic) for the first line and a repeated E (dominant) for the second. This quasi-recitativo melodic style is an important characteristic in the music of Fauré, Chausson, and Duparc, and is used even more extensively by Debussy. It reinforces the trancelike quality of this beautiful song.

"Soupir" is one of the most touching songs ever written. Each phrase in the accompaniment is a sigh, each line of the poem by Sully Prudhomme a cry of pain. The exquisite harmonies, be they minor, major, diminished, or augmented, seem laden with sorrow. A brief piano introduction sets the mood and announces the main harmonic devices to be used throughout the song: frequent pedal points* on the dominant (this is characteristic of Duparc and Fauré), the extension of the dominant-seventh chord by adding thirds (D, F sharp, A, C, E sharp, for instance), and the creating of chords by

---

*The retention over several measures of a single root note, usually in the bass.

holding notes which have been sounded sequentially. Sections of harmonic stasis alternate with periods of constant modulation—another characteristic of Duparc.

The singer's first two lines are derived from dominant chords. Their downward curves echo the sorrow in the words: "Never to see her or hear her / Never to say her name." The end is even more mournful than the beginning as the words conclude "But always with a love ever more tender / Always to love her.   Always." The final "Toujours" is separated from the other words by a two-measure piano interlude. When it is finally heard—a heartbroken whisper over a surprising major chord—the coldest heart must be moved.

The title of the next song, "Lamento," is its own best description. Its minor mode and descending chromatic melody are as heavy with grief as its text by Théophile Gautier. The poem subtly evokes the visual—the tomb is white, the tree casts a shadow, the dove is pale, the evening wears a black cloak—there is no color, only chiaroscuro. The words are remarkable too for their use of sound—the onomatopoeia of "roucoulement" ("cooing"); the inner rhymes of "tombe," "l'ombre," "colombe"; the deliberate repetition of sound in "Chante son chant."

Taking his cue from the text, Duparc uses repetition to create a hypnotic effect. The first four notes of the falling chromatic melody in the piano introduction become the vocal line in five key spots, and the piano repeats this beautifully harmonized phrase in five subsequent interludes. Since the song is short, this one musical idea permeates and characterizes it. Its return at the end of the song, "Bien doucement" ("Very softly"), brings the song full cycle.

Unlike the three songs discussed above, "La Vague et la Cloche" was originally conceived for voice and orchestra. To make Duparc's piano rendition effective, the pianist must therefore make the accompaniment as orchestral as possible: the surging figures in the bass must be massive and sonorous, the frequent tremolos should imitate shimmering strings in full vibrato, and the dynamic range must extend from a pianissimo to a fortissimo.

The poem, by François Coppée, describes a nightmarish fantasy of being adrift without a lantern on a stormy sea. The piano's arpeggiated figure suggests the billowing waves (La Vague means the sea or the waves; it can also mean vagueness, a connotation probably intended at the end of the poem; La Cloche is the bell). The music exudes a chilling sense of foreboding as the words say "The ocean spat its foam on my forehead / And the wind froze me with horror to my entrails." One is immediately reminded of "The Descent into the Maelstrom" by Edgar Allan Poe, a poet much admired by writers and musicians of this era.

The piano's loud, sweeping scales imitate the turbulent waters until an ominous drop to a pianissimo sets off the words: "Then everything changed . . . The sea and its black whirl subsided." A tremendous crescendo brings us to the climactic moment when the boat collapses beneath our hero's feet and he finds himself thrown on an old bell tower. As he clutches the rapidly swinging bell to save himself, the music depicts its wild oscillations, its clangorous sound, and the continuing roar of the ocean. After all the sound and fury the song ends not with a bang, but not exactly with a whimper either. It has all been a dream, but dream is a metaphor for life.

Throughout this most dramatic of Duparc's songs, its harmonic structure gives it cohesiveness and unity. The logical flow of its musical ideas effectively sees it through its many changes of mood.

Claude Debussy
(1862–1918)

Of the composers related by the shared artistic ideals of the late nineteenth and early twentieth centuries in France—an aesthetic influenced by Symbolist poets and Impressionist painters in particular and by the highly cultivated atmosphere of Paris before the First World War in general—none can match the creative power of Claude Debussy. Debussy was a seminal figure in the realm of piano technique, adding new sounds and colors to the vocabulary of pianism in his *Estampes, Images,* and *Préludes.* Not since Chopin had the piano's resources been exploited in such an innovative manner. In symphonic works such as *L'Après-midi d'un faune, Ibéria, Nuages,* and *La Mer* his haunting harmonies and shimmering orchestration created a new orchestral atmosphere, and his opera *Pelléas et Mélisande,* the epitome of musical Impressionism, represents the ultimate union of words and music.

Debussy's fifty-five songs span his creative years, the first appearing in 1876 and the last in 1915. Their emotional range extends from the passionately erotic ("La Chevelure," "Le Jet d'eau," "C'est l'extase") to the gaily insouciant ("Mandoline," "Fantoches," "Pantomime"), the pastoral ("Voici que le Printemps"), the religious ("Ballade que fait Villon à la Requeste de sa Mère pour Prier Nostre-Dame"), and the bitterly antiwar ("Noël des enfants qui n'ont plus de maisons"). Of the early songs we shall discuss "Mandoline" and "Apparition"; of the *Cinq Poèmes de Baudelaire* (1887–89), "Harmonie du Soir"; from *Ariettes Oubliées,* "C'est l'Extase"; from *Fêtes Galantes I,* "Clair de Lune"; from *Proses Lyriques,* "De Rêve"; from *Fêtes Galantes II,* "Colloque Sentimental"; and from *Trois Ballades de François Villon,* "Ballade que fait Villon à la Requeste de sa Mère pour Prier Nostre-Dame."

"Mandoline" is the first of many songs written by Debussy to texts of Paul Verlaine. In fact, of his fifty-five songs, eighteen owe their inspiration to that brilliant poet. Since Verlaine's poetry has the same fluidity of form, absence of rhetoric, and mixture of the vague and the precise that we associate with Impressionistic art and music, Debussy's affinity for his works is quite natural.

The song opens with a brightly struck single note (G) preceded by a grace note which adds to the sonority and the "ping." After the attention-getting sound dies away, mandolin-like chords begin a sprightly introduction. The discordant A's and G's in the chords are reminiscent of an instrument tuning up, but by the second line all is harmony. The singer has a sensuous chromatic descent on one long syllable ("chan*teuses*") while the piano plays unexpected chords. The word "tendre" brings a change to a sweet and tender mood but strummed chords and gay "la, la, las" in the text bring the song to a carefree conclusion. The last note is like the first—a little "ping" on the dominant.

"Apparition" is regarded as one of the most important works of Symbolist poet Stéphane Mallarmé. In it one sees the universal *correspondance* first expressed by Baudelaire: the moon is sad, flowers are calm, sighs are white, there is an odor of sadness, white bouquets are perfumed with stars.

Debussy's setting is quite ambitious, making it the most important of his early songs. The opening section is celestial, ethereal. The piano begins with a shimmering figure on the tonic triad colored by the sound of the flatted second (F natural in the key of E major). The voice enters on the dominant and dreamily intones its first six syllables on that one note. This stylistic device—a repeated melodic note surrounded by lovely harmonies—is one of Debussy's most frequently encountered characteristics. The complexity of the opening rhythm—3/4 in the voice against 9/8 in the piano part—is another Debussy trademark.

As the voice leaves the dominant note, it climbs chromatically and then undulates. An atmospheric use of chromaticism and floating augmented chords characterizes the whole section. At the key line "It was the blessed day of your first kiss," the music becomes warm and unabashedly romantic, with full rich chords in the piano supporting the impassioned melody. The cooler, more ephemeral mood alternates with the effusive romanticism, until finally one senses the earthiness of human passion transfigured into celestial ecstasy. The song fades away with quiet delicacy.

An equally beautiful poem, this time by Charles Baudelaire, provides the text for "Harmonie du Soir" ("Harmony of the Evening"). The third line of the poem, "Les sons et les parfums tournent dans l'air du soir" ("The sounds and scents turn in the evening air"), also inspired one of Debussy's piano preludes. Although the song is in B major (in the key for high voice) Debussy begins with a C sharp minor triad. The second measure introduces a characteristic little figure, triplet sixteenth notes, which probably represents things "turning in the air." Of the first ten notes of the vocal line, all but the first two are at whole-tone intervals (use of the whole-tone scale is so closely associated with Debussy that other composers use it only at the risk of sounding imitative!). The enchanting atmosphere of the song is created by enharmonic changes, alternation of chromatic and whole-tone melodic phrases, and exquisite harmonies. The complicated structure of the poem is reflected in the music—line II is repeated as line I of the second stanza while line IV of stanza I becomes line III of stanza II, and so forth—and yet the music flows naturally from phrase to phrase. The lines "Le violon frémit comme un coeur qu'on afflige; / Valse mélancolique et langoureux vertige" ("The violin shudders like a wounded heart; / Melancholy waltz and languorous vertigo!") are too beautiful not to be quoted!

A wry story lies behind the title of the six-song collection to texts of Paul Verlaine called *Ariettes Oubliées (Forgotten Airs).* Originally published under the title *Ariettes* in 1888, they were unnoticed by public or critics until after the success of *Pelléas et Mélisande* some fifteen years later. Consequently upon their republication Debussy added the word "Oubliées" to their name.

"C'est l'Extase," the first song of the group, is an unabashed description of the languorous fatigue that follows erotic passion. Debussy's mood indication, "slow and caressing," deliberately underscores the physical connotation of the words. The piano's opening chords are heavy with sensuality. The singer, beginning with a slow-moving, downward scale fragment, dreamily murmurs "C'est l'extase langoureuse / C'est la fatigue amoureuse" ("This is languid ecstasy / This is erotic fatigue"). The melodic line becomes almost static as the singer uses a series of repeated notes to describe sensations like ". . . the trembling of the woods / In the embrace of the breezes." In the middle section, where there is much more motion, the highly chromatic accompaniment sometimes clashes momentarily with the equally chromatic melodic line. The beautiful words "O le frêle frais murmure / Cela gazouille et susurre" ("Oh, the frail cool murmur / It twitters and whispers"), with their soft, sibilant sounds, are passed over quickly in this section, and the music becomes quite animated. A passionate climax is reached a few measures before the end, but the final lines return to the languid, hushed atmosphere of the beginning.

Verlaine's poem "Clair de Lune" inspired two settings by Debussy and one by Fauré; furthermore one can assume that its words lie behind Debussy's lovely piano piece from *Suite Bergamasque* that bears the same name. Debussy's first vocal setting of "Clair de Lune" (ca. 1883) is a rather immature effort, but the second, which we discuss here (1892), is comparable in inspiration and execution to the masterpiece of Fauré (see page 130). In many respects the two songs are similar—each begins with an independent piano prelude and there is almost total agreement on rhythmic emphasis and verbal placement.

There are many exquisite harmonic changes in Debussy's song. The first occurs between measures 7 and 8 under the word "bergamasques," where the piano's chords seem to be lifted harmonically while the singer's melodic line falls. In the very next measure another gorgeous harmonic lift to an augmented chord underlies an insistent repeated note in the vocal part. The constantly soaring accompaniment leaps again in measure 11 but finally, under "déguisements" in bar 12, there is a return to the principal tonality. The key line of the poem, "Au calme clair de lune" ("In the calm moonlight"), is set off by a ravishing, serenely ethereal melodic phrase, and the song ends with harmonies of gossamer purity.

"De Rêve" is the first of the four *Proses Lyriques* for which Debussy wrote the words as well as the music. Debussy had a considerable reputation as a witty and astute writer of musical criticism; these four poems and the text he wrote for "Nöel pour les enfants qui n'ont plus de maisons" mark him as a poet of distinction. The imagery in "De Rêve" is striking: "La tête emperlée" ("the pearl-covered head"); "des hanches fleurissantes" ("blossoming or flowering hips''); trees which "fleurent leur belles feuilles d'or" ("shed like tears their beautiful golden leaves"), and so forth. The way in which Debussy gradually makes us aware of the subject of his dream, from the earliest suggestion of ancient mode of dress ("la tête emperlée") to the precise picture of knights seeking the Holy Grail, makes the poem effective even from a purely narrative point of view.

From the opening bars of the song it is clear that Debussy has written the ideal text for his own characteristic style of composition. The piano begins with an arpeggiated augmented chord, and there are suggestions of the whole-tone scale in melody. Throughout the song there are long pauses in the vocal line, pauses filled with beautifully atmospheric piano interludes. Debussy's favorite rhythmic device —regular eighth notes against triplet eighth notes—is heard in the andantino section. Later this becomes sixteenth notes against triplet eighth notes, which emphasizes the quickened pace.

Although Debussy deliberately obscures the tonality of the song, the opening key signature (F sharp and C sharp for high voice) leads us to assume B minor as the main key. Frequent modulations within sections and changes in key signature to B major, C major, back to B minor and finally to F sharp major weaken still further the claims of any one tonal center. Even when the final key has been established, notes foreign to its triad keep the harmonies suitably hazy for the concluding words: "Strange sighs rise under the trees. / My soul is from an ancient dream which embraces you!"

"Colloque Sentimental" is the last song by Debussy to be based on a poem by Verlaine, and a more disturbing text is hard to imagine. In it the ephemeral nature of erotic love is treated in stark, grim fashion. The title is ironic, for the principal protagonist in this dialogue for solo voice is unable to arouse a sentimental or even nostalgic response from her former lover.

To convey the meaning of the text the singer must project two different characters. While the questions and answers alternate this is not too difficult, but in lines 9 and 10 two questions are asked before the single-word response—"No"—is delivered: "Does your heart still beat at my name?/ Do you always see my soul in your dreams?/ No."

The song opens with a brief piano introduction based for three of its four measures on a whole-tone scale. The chill and lonely mood is conveyed by the emptiness of the single notes in the first bar. The unaccompanied opening vocal phrase is followed by a bleak intoned line, nine of whose ten syllables are on one repeated note. Throughout the introductory narrative, which describes the two lonely and chilled specters with dead eyes and slack lips, changes of pitch in the melodic line are limited.

Toward the end of the introductory section, a note is heard in the piano part—a C in the key for high voice—which becomes an extremely significant feature of the music. It is present in every measure of the central section of the song (the entire dialogue) and is almost always used as a syncopated rhythmic figure. Sometimes this insistent note is played alone and sometimes it is buried in the chords, but wherever possible it should be heard.

There is an epilogue to the brief drama and a fade-out ending, neither of which alleviates the gloom. The concluding lines are "Thus they walked in the wild oats / And only the night heard their words."

For the "Ballade que fait Villon à la Requeste de sa Mère pour Prier Nostre-Dame," Debussy turned to the words of fifteenth-century writer François Villon. From 1904 to 1910, the year in which this song appeared, Debussy set to music two texts by Villon's contemporary, Charles d'Orléans, four by the early seventeenth-century poet Tristan L'Hermite, and the *Trois Ballades de François Villon*, of which this is the second. It is undoubtedly the most convincing religious statement to be found among Debussy's songs, inspired as it is by the simple faith of Villon's words.

As the title states, Villon wrote the Ballade at his mother's request, for her to use as a prayer to the Virgin Mary. It is his legacy to her (as stated in *Le Testament*, his principal work) in remorse for having caused her so much grief by his wild behavior. The Ballade expresses feelings of unworthiness, guilt, hope for forgiveness, and tears of contrition with such poignancy that one feels that the prayer is as much for himself as for his pure-hearted mother.

Like all ballades, this one has a refrain which is repeated at the end of every other four-line stanza. The words, "En ceste foy je veuil vivre et mourir" ("In this faith I wish to live and to die")—the spelling is Old French but the pronunciation scarcely differs from the modern—are always sung to the same music, a device which provides structural unity for the long song.

The song begins with a simple unaccompanied melodic line. The chords which follow are solemn and archaic, and the melody for "Recevez moy, vostre humble chrestienne" ("Receive me, your humble Christian") is like a church-service chant. Other references to religious services—bell-like notes in the accompaniment, parallel fifths and octaves (forbidden by eighteenth- and nineteenth-century rules of harmonization but frequently encountered in church music of the Middle Ages), and intoned phrases with many syllables sung on one repeated note—permeate the song with antique atmosphere.

To many critics this song and its two companions represent the apex of Debussy's genius as composer of art songs.

Limited space has prevented us from discussing the three *Chansons de Bilitis* (1897) and the three *Chansons de France* (1904), additional high points in the output of this remarkable composer.

Maurice Ravel, Erik Satie,
(1875–1937) (1866–1925)

Darius Milhaud, and Francis Poulenc
(1892–1974) (1899–1963)

Despite the fact that creative artists are often basically apolitical, major historical events—especially those of a cataclysmic nature—do influence the artistic zeitgeist of an era. France, devastated beyond her worst apprehensions by the combination of hand-to-hand combat and modern weaponry that wracked Europe from 1914 to 1918, was irrevocably changed by World War I; French musicians could not help but be affected by these changes.

Of the French composers whose lives span the pre– and post–World War I eras, Maurice Ravel is the most important. Usually bracketed with Debussy, his works show similarities to and differences from the works of the older composer. Their piano music shares many coloristic and harmonic characteristics; in that area of composition Ravel's influence on Debussy was almost as great as Debussy's on Ravel. In their songs they follow quite separate routes, Ravel emphasizing classical line, folk elements, and dry wit in his vocal works. His early songs, such as the three-part cycle *Shéhérazade* (1903), are still awash with Impressionistic color and Oriental exoticism, but after World War I he turned from what he called "the luxury art" of Impressionism, becoming more restrained, more concerned with form, more abstract.

Although *Shéhérazade* was first composed for solo voice and piano and only later orchestrated by Ravel (this is typical of Ravel's composition technique—most of his orchestral works were first conceived as piano pieces), the orchestration now seems an integral part of the concept, particularly in the opening section, "Asie." Here the singer recites the splendors of the Orient to a background enlivened by tambourines, a variety of bells and gongs, harp, and rich strings. The lush, undulating melody evokes the opulence of the mysterious East.

The second section of *Shéhérazade*, "La Flûte enchantée," is a duet for voice and flute supported by orchestra. The words tell of a young slave listening to her lover's flute while her master sleeps. The flute weaves graceful arabesques around the vocal melody.

The cycle has a sad ending, "L' Indifférent," in which melancholy, yearning, and disappointment are expressed. Of the three sections it is the least colorful.

"Vocalise en forme d'habanera" is another exotic vocal work from this era (1907). Its wordless melody is sensuous and lush; its Spanish rhythms and atmospheric orchestration weave a voluptuous spell. The voice, with its coloratura acrobatics and long trills, often sounds instrumental.

In the same year, 1907, Ravel published a set of five charming little *Histoires Naturelles* (*Nature Stories*) based on texts of Jules Renard (renard, coincidentally, is the French word for fox!). These wry, typically Gallic tales describe in turn "Le Paon" ("The Peacock"), "Le Grillon" ("The Cricket"), "Le Cygne" ("The Swan"), "Le Martin-pêcheur" ("The Kingfisher"), and "La Pintade" ("The Guinea Hen").

Ravel sets the words naturally, with no undue ornamentation. The only special effects allowed in the music are those
which help portray the animals—sharp seconds for the quar-
relsome guinea hen, a descending interval in imitation of the
peacock's strident cry (his fiancée has stood him up and he's
angry!), shimmering arpeggiated chords to describe the
swan gliding on the lake, and so forth. The comic touches
and overall good humor of the songs never obscure the genuine beauty and richness of the music, which places the cycle
firmly in the sphere of "serious" music.

Ravel was neither the first nor the last to compose
"animal" songs. Emmanuel Chabrier (1841–1894), a composer of wit, verve, and considerable brilliance, wrote his
"farmyard" pieces—"Pastorale des petits cochons roses,"
"Ballade des gros dindons," "Villanelle des petits canards,"
and so forth ("Pastorale of the Little Red Pigs," Ballad of
the Fat Turkeys," "Villanelle of the Little Ducks," and so
forth) based on texts by Edmond Rostand, the author of
Cyrano de Bergerac, in 1890. Camille Saint-Saëns's *Carnaval des animaux,* an orchestral piece with two pianos in
which "The Scale-Playing Pianists" are listed among the
strange animals, was composed in 1886. Continuing the
tradition in the next generation we find Poulenc's droll *Le
Bestiaire* (1919, poems by Guillaume Apollinaire) in which
we meet a camel, a goat, a dolphin, a carp, a crayfish, and a
grasshopper.

Ravel, called upon for various reasons at various times
to harmonize folk tunes, wrote *Five Popular Greek Melodies*
(1907), *Four Popular Songs*—one Spanish, one French, one
Italian, and one Hebrew (1910), and *Two Hebrew Melodies*
(1914). These are all remarkably evocative of their native
lands, for Ravel always allows the original flavor of the traditional songs to predominate. Sometimes, as in "Enigma Eter-
nelle" (one of the Hebrew melodies), the accompaniments

are highly sophisticated, contrasting markedly with the folk melodies. In this instance Ravel uses complex polytonal chord combinations. More often the harmonizations are deliberately limited and simple.

Unique in the vocal chamber-music repertoire is Ravel's gorgeous three-part cycle, *Chansons madécasses* (1925–26), settings of native poems translated into French by Evariste Parny, scored for voice, flute, cello, and piano. Over a pulsating solo cello figure of great rhythmic complexity, the voice enters, calling the name "Nahandove." It is her lover, waiting for her on the bed of leaves, flowers, and sweet-smelling herbs that he has prepared. The piano replaces the cello as the pace quickens and his excitement mounts. The vocal line is very limited in scope and all is hushed expectancy. The cello reenters followed by the chirping flute, and the vocal tessitura rises. Finally she has arrived; her kisses penetrate his soul, her caresses burn his senses. "Arrête, ou je vais mourir," he cries ("Stop or I'll die"). This is of course the climax of the song, after which passion is replaced by gentle languor. The flute plays long low notes and then disappears while the cello repeats its original hypnotic figure. "You'll return this evening, won't you, Nahandove, Oh, beautiful Nahandove! . . ."

The second song of this cycle is angry and bitter. "Beware of the whites!" cries the voice over biting discordant chords. In tense declamatory style the ugly story of betrayal of the naive and friendly natives by colonists is related. The music's pounding repetitious chords have the hypnotic power of jungle drums. The refrain, "Méfiez-vous des blancs" ("Beware of the whites"), lances the soul.

The third song is somewhat anticlimactic after the passion and dramatic intensity of the first two. It describes in gentle, quiet music how sweet it is to rest under a shady tree during the heat of the day. As the evening breeze rises and the moon begins to shine, he says to her, "Go, and prepare the meal." These last few homely words are unaccompanied and totally ingenuous.

Ravel's last compositions were the three songs entitled *Don Quichotte à Dulcinée* (1932). Originally conceived for a movie for which Ravel was to have written the entire score (actually Ravel's music was not used on the project, having been replaced by a score by Jacques Ibert), the songs give Ravel a chance to exploit the Spanish rhythms so natural to him (his mother was Spanish). The first, "Chanson romanesque," is a guajira, in which 6/8 and 3/4 measures alternate. The 3/4 sections sound very waltzlike, and the 6/8 sections are enlivened by amusingly discordant chords. The words describe Don Quichotte's ardor for Dulcinée, for whom he would gladly die.

"Chanson épique," the second song, is a zarzico, which is characterized by 5/4 meter. The music is quite serious and sincerely religious, as Don Quichotte prays to Saints Michael and George for the "knightly grace" to defend Dulcinée's honor and beauty.

The final song is, as the title states, a drinking song ("Chanson à Boire"). Rhythmically it is a Spanish dance, but in it Ravel's Gallic wit comes through the heavy Spanish flavor.

Before moving on to Satie and "Les Six," the next generation of French composers, we must at least mention a few of the talented writers who added to the immense song literature of the turn of the century. Of greatest international renown was Albert Roussel (1869–1937) whose piano music is occasionally heard in concert today. Of more limited talent was the sole woman composer of the group, Cécile Chami-

nade (1857–1944). More frequently encountered in song recitals are the quite lovely works of Reynaldo Hahn (1875–
1947) and Georges Hüe (1858–1948).

    Although Erik Satie's dates (1866–1925) make him al-
most an exact contemporary of Debussy (1862–1918), in no
way did he share the aesthetic ideals associated with Debussy and other Impressionists. Unlike Ravel, he did not go
through an extended Impressionist stage; from his earliest
works, which were influenced primarily by medieval plainsong, he was opposed to the hazy wash of color created by
the atmospheric harmonies chosen by Fauré, Chausson, Duparc, and Debussy. He was equally antagonistic to the Romantic and Symbolist poetry chosen by these composers,
preferring dry, epigrammatic, tongue-in-cheek texts. To
show his disdain for sentimentality and pomposity, he created the "café-concert" or music-hall style, which utilizes the
perky rhythms, sassy words, and bright colors of popular
music.
    Interestingly enough, Satie's antipathy for the Debussy
idiom was by no means reciprocated. Debussy was fond
enough of Satie's *Gymnopédies* to orchestrate them, and
they are as familiar to us in that form as in their original
version for piano solo.
    Debussy's favorite painters were the Impressionists, for
whom color is far more important than line. Satie, on the
other hand, became associated with Picasso during his Cubist period, when line—fragmented and then reintegrated in
unfamiliar ways—took precedence over color (many of the
Cubist paintings of Picasso, Braque, and Juan Gris are in
shades of brown and gray, and many deal with musical subjects). Satie attempted to implement Cubist ideals in music,
using simple, familiar chords in unexpected contexts, as

Cubist painters used familiar forms in odd juxtapositions and superimpositions. While Cubist methods produced highly sophisticated paintings, in Satie's music they created a rather childlike innocence, undermined by Satie's satiric verbal commentaries.

Like César Franck, Satie is important more for the strong influence he exerted over the next generation than for his actual compositions, which were few and often facetious. His most important vocal work is the austere "Death of Socrates" section from *Socrate,* a setting for four soprano soloists and chamber orchestra of three of Plato's dialogues (in French translation). Most of his solo songs are in the music-hall style which so enchanted Poulenc, Milhaud, and dozens of other younger composers.

In 1917, in Paris, author Jean Cocteau, a friend of Picasso and Satie, attempted to band together a few young composers who, in their mutual regard for Satie, would acknowledge the older composer's influence on their work. Known as "Les Six," this loosely knit group consisted of Arthur Honegger (1892–1955), Louis Durey (b. 1888), Georges Auric (b. 1899), Germaine Tailleferre (b. 1892) Darius Milhaud (1892–1974), and Francis Poulenc (1899–1963). It soon became evident that, aside from a rather Puckish sense of humor, the only characteristic these six friends really shared was an adventurous, iconoclastic individuality which made it impossible for them to function as a group or to adhere to any external guidelines for their work. Honegger, who didn't really care much for Satie's music, was the first to disassociate himself from the group, followed soon after by Durey who stopped composing in the 1920s. What remained of the association was their friendship and an ongoing interest is each other's professional activities. Of "The Six" the two most important songwriters are Milhaud and, above all, Poulenc.

A glance at the catalog of his works confirms Milhaud's reputation as one of the most prolific composers of the twentieth century. Operas, ballets, incidental music for films and stage works, radio music, choral music, orchestral works, military band music, jazz band music, concerti, music for voice and orchestra, chamber music, piano solos, pieces for two and four pianos, organ music, and hundreds of songs were created by this industrious, versatile, and facile composer. His best-known works, such as the orchestral suite from the ballet *La Création du Monde* (1923), utilize jazz rhythms most effectively; in *Le Boeuf sur le toit* (1919), another popular ballet suite, Brazilian folk and popular music is much in evidence.

The many facets of Milhaud's musical personality are well represented in his songs, which range from frivolous settings for voice and chamber orchestra of trade catalogs (*Machines agricoles,* 1919, and *Catalogue des fleurs,* 1920) to warmly lyrical evocations of Jewish folklore (*Poèmes juifs,* 1916). The versatility of his technique is also apparent in his songs. Let us compare, for instance, two similar lullabies, one from *Chants populaires Hébraïques* (1925) and the other from *Poèmes juifs.** In the former, the singer's melody and the outer voices of the piano accompaniment all focus on the minor triad. (The vocal line also features the flatted second for Oriental flavor.) However the moving inner voice of the piano part supplies notes foreign to the triad, thereby transforming the simple harmonies into complex, often discordant

---

*Milhaud took pride and pleasure in his Jewish origins. Aside from the two sets of songs mentioned above, he composed a "Hymn to Zion" (1925), "Daily Prayers for the Use of Jews of Comtat Venaissin (1927), five songs for Rosh Hashanah (1933), two Palestinian folk songs (1937), and a cantata called *Crown of Glory* for the centennial anniversary of the synagogue of Aix-en-Provence (1940).

combinations. In the latter, called "Chant de Nourrice" ("The Nurse's Song"), Milhaud eschews obvious Oriental effects. Instead, in this deceptively simple song, we have a complex harmonic situation in which the left hand of the piano plays in one key for long stretches while the right hand and vocal line move chromatically above the droning bass. It is not until the tenth measure of the song that the two parts coalesce on the tonic (B major) and that meeting is brief. For the great majority of the time the song is bitonal—in two keys simultaneously. Milhaud shows great skill in handling this bitonality, and the resultant sound combination is very beautiful indeed.

The closer in time we come to our own era, the more dangerous it becomes to assess the worth of composers. Nevertheless at this time it seems that the most serious and lasting contribution by the post-Satie group was made by Francis Poulenc. Of his instrumental music, his saucy sonatas for piano four-hands, flute and piano, clarinet and piano, clarinet and bassoon; his trio for oboe, bassoon, and piano; his concerto for two pianos; and his sextet for flute, oboe, clarinet, bassoon, horn, and piano are all frequently encountered in concert. His finest music is undoubtedly to be found in his "Gloria" and in the powerful opera *Dialogues des Carmélites* (1957).

Poulenc found in the song the ideal outlet for his spontaneous melodic inventiveness and his unique comic gift. While many of his songs are tender and delicate ("C'est le joli printemps" from *Chansons Villageoises,* 1942, for example) and a few are gravely philosophical ("Le Mendiant" from the same cycle), most range from playful to downright funny. It is almost impossible to hear tenor Pierre Bernac, Poulenc's favorite interpreter, sing the wildly comic patter songs "Chanson de la fille frivole," "Le gars qui vont à la fête," or

"Chanson du clair tamis" (all from *Chansons Villageoises,* texts by Maurice Fombeure) without chuckling. This same fine singer, for whom Poulenc wrote many of his songs, projects just as effectively the sophisticated irony of the texts of Guillaume Apollinaire, Poulenc's favorite poet, in "Hotel" and "Sanglots" from *Banalités* (the two cycles mentioned above may be heard sung by Bernac with Poulenc at the keyboard on a Columbia record—ML 4333).

One of Poulenc's wryest songs is "Avant le cinéma" (Apollinaire—1931) which, in its brief fifty-second duration, admonishes everyone to go to the cinema for the sake of culture. In contrast is the extended, serious, religious statement, "Hymne" (1949), based on a text by seventeenth-century playwright Jean Racine. In "Le Souris" (Apollinaire, 1956) we find one of the odd, unexpected final chords which are a Poulenc trademark. The cycle *Chansons gaillardes* (1926), based on light, often bawdy, anonymous seventeenth-century poems, is mostly in music-hall style.

Regardless of the intent of an individual piece—be it bawdy, religious, grave, or comic—never do we find in Poulenc's songs the ephemeral harmonic sensitivity or the passionate involvement of the Impressionist composers. For Poulenc and the others of "Les Six," effusive romanticism and excessive refinement were passé and to be avoided.

Nationalism, Part I:
The Russians

During the Middle Ages all of Western civilization was united by the traditions of Christianity. Educated people could exchange ideas in a common tongue, Latin. Once musical notation was widely known, a Mass composed in Paris could be sung in Saxony, Venice, London, or anywhere else in Europe or England. Despite physical difficulties composers and painters traveled widely, often gaining international renown. New ideas spread quickly and freely.

Even when working outside the confines of the Church and in "vulgate" languages, artists and musicians thought in universal terms, ascribing little importance to regional differences. This far-reaching cosmopolitanism lasted for many centuries: Händel, born in Germany, influenced by his sojourn in Italy, created most of his important works in England; Italian-born Domenico Scarlatti flourished in Spain; Mozart was as comfortable in Italian opera as he was in German; none thought of himself as a specifically national composer.

When eighteenth-century musicians such as Haydn occasionally did use indigenous folk material, it was incorporated into the internationally accepted style of the period. With the rise of nationalism, a primarily nineteenth-century concept, artists and musicians began to exploit the peculiar characteristics of their own lands—their native folk cultures —emphasizing the historically rooted individualistic aspects of their arts. This new preoccupation influenced some areas far more than others. In Germany, the strong tradition of symphonic and vocal music, which predated the actual formation of the German nation, dulled the impact of new nationalistic tendencies in music, although composers such as Brahms were quite attracted to folk tunes. In France, the major European nation with the longest history as a political entity, the nineteenth-century blossoming of French-language poetry stimulated the golden age of Fauré, Chausson, Duparc, Debussy, and Ravel, but this had little to do with native folk traditions. In fact when French composers wanted "local color," they usually preferred to seek it in Spain. Of course there were German, French, and Italian styles, but these were the result of centuries of natural development, during which locally composed works, indigenous folk music, and compositions from other areas enriched one another.

It was primarily in countries such as Russia, Spain, England, Norway, and Finland, regions which lacked ongoing traditions of "serious" music (Russia, Norway, Finland) or lands in which circumstances had caused a long hiatus in musical creativity (England, Spain), that the impact of nationalism was strongest. In this chapter we shall discuss the most important nineteenth-century Russian nationalist composers, Glinka, Dargomizhsky, Borodin and Moussorgsky, and their "internationalist" compatriots, Tchaikovsky and Rachmaninov.

Russian soil proved most fertile for the development of musical nationalism. Isolated from European culture by her vast size and forbidding weather, Russia was virtually untouched by the Renaissance. By the eighteenth century, when contact with European civilization was fully established, she had developed an enormous inferiority complex regarding all aspects of culture: the upper classes preferred to converse in French, feeling that the Russian language was too coarse; opera and painting were imported from France and Italy and symphonic music from Germany; anyone who wanted to study art or music went abroad. Although there was a widespread and rich indigenous folk-art tradition, it was enjoyed only by the peasantry, who knew nothing of the imported culture of their masters.

When a few early nineteenth-century Russians attempted to express themselves musically, their slavish imitation of European music led to unconvincing, second-rate compositions. It was soon apparent that an exploration of native music was the only viable alternative.

The first Russian composer successfully to combine European technique and Russian folk music was Mikhail Glinka (1804–1857). Most of Glinka's childhood was spent on his family's country estate, where he became steeped in peasant song and lore. From 1817 on he was subjected to all the usual European influences—a German piano teacher, an Italian singing master, sojourns in Milan, Rome, Naples, Paris, and Spain. He gradually became convinced that the only hope for nonderivative creativity among Russian composers was inspiration from native Russian authors (he composed seven songs to texts by Aleksander Pushkin and used the poems of many lesser-known Russian poets) and folk music. Although the influence of his Italian training can still be heard in such songs as "Doubt" and "The Lark," in his operas *A Life for the Tsar* (1836) and *Russlan and Ludmila* (1842), we hear the beginnings of a genuine school of Russian music.

Alexander Dargomizhsky (1813–1869), composer of the opera *The Stone Guest* (Pushkin's version of the Don Juan story), wrote approximately ninety songs, most of them characteristically Russian in style. They range in emotional content from drama to humor, many satirizing the pomposity of the Russian petty official. Typical are the bitter "I Am Grieving," whose text by Mikhail Lermontov tells of the jealous, rejected lover who grieves because "he" is happy with his new love, and "Look, Darling Maiden," a gay little strophic song to an anonymous folk text.

If Glinka and Dargomizhsky were the pioneers of Russian song, the masters were undoubtedly Alexander Borodin (1833–1887) and Modest Moussorgsky (1839–1881). Each had a distinctive style based on empirical, coloristic harmonies and the speech rhythms of the Russian language. Moussorgsky was more adamant in his avoidance of set melodies; he favored the irregular, asymmetrical rhythms of Russian folk tunes and the declamatory style of natural, albeit musical speech.

Borodin's earliest songs (1853–55), based on texts by German poet Heine and incorporating cello obbligato, were quite derivative, but those of 1867–68, written to his own poems, show his mature style. These include the remarkable "Sleeping Beauty," "Sea Princess," "Song of the Dark Forest," and "The False Note," each of which shows his fine lyrical gift and his imaginative use of bold, fresh harmonies. "Sleeping Beauty" and "Song of the Dark Forest" feature throbbing, unresolved major seconds, an effect which intrigued Debussy and other French Impressionists. The former has a swaying, nurserylike tune, with a gentle refrain ("Sleep, sleep"). Mysterious, ominous, atmospheric effects accompany the words "Lo, the forest dark has stirred"; a declamatory, repeated-note vocal line, similar to those used by Debussy, alternates with the more lyrical nursery-tune.

"The False Note" is a seventeen-bar epigram in which one note is heard throughout. Its brief poem has a cynical last line and the music is equally sardonic. Dedicated to Moussorgsky it expresses doubt over a young lady's protestations of love, in which the author senses "a false note." The punch line is ". . . she understood this well."

Later songs include many satirical sketches such as "Pride" (text by A. K. Tolstoy, 1885) in which pomposity is described in words and music. The tune is folk-derived, and the many amusing touches in the accompaniment include "Volga Boatman"–like chords. In epic ballad style is "The Sea" (1870, own words) which depicts the stormy, raging ocean. This song, with its tempestuous accompaniment, was also admired by Debussy, who compared it favorably to his own "La Mer."

Of Moussorgsky's songs the most highly regarded are the four *Songs and Dances of Death*, composed in 1875–77 to texts by Golenishev-Kutuzov. Each of these dramatic scenes portrays Death in a different guise. In the first, "Trepak," Death lures a poor old drunken peasant with the words "Rest, here your sleep will be deep and endless. / See, I will warm and bed you down in the soft snow . . ." After a brief narrative opening describing the barren woodlands, soft tremolos in the accompaniment hint at the storm soon to come. The sad folk tune begins its lament, continuing with little variation throughout the song, while the accompaniment expresses in pictorial terms the howling wind, and the heavy dance which unites Death and the peasant. Moussorgsky's sympathy for the Russian peasant who had only recently (1861) been freed from serfdom is evident in his choice of texts and in the libretto for the opera *Boris Godunov* which he wrote himself. In "Trepak" the poet says, "Poor serf, distressed, oppressed, and friendless . . ."

The second song of the set, "Lullaby," is a dialogue between Death and a mother whose child lies ill. The introductory narrative is sung in recitativo, declamatory style, after which, in more lyrical melody, Death tries to convince the mother that he should take the baby. It is Death who sings the tender refrain, "Hush-a-bye, baby, my own," lovely soft-sounding Russian words.

In "Serenade" Death woos a young maiden by promising her eternal youth and beauty. With a lover's ardor he praises her, saying, "How you arouse my desire." His exultant last words, spoken as much as sung (the score indication is parlando), are "Your lover is calling, listen . . . Be still . . . You are mine!" Much of the music is heavy with repetitious melodic phrases and accompanying chords. In the final measures an ostinato on the tonic (C sharp) emphasizes this hypnotically monotonous droning.

The last of the set, called "The General," sums up the futility of war, for Death conquers all on the battlefield. Moussorgsky incorporates part of the Polish Revolutionary March in the music, bringing reality into the song. The opening section is typically military with vigorous triplets marking the 4/4 beat. A more contemplative section describes the lonely field at night when the troops have withdrawn, leaving only the moans of the wounded to disturb the silence. Death enters to a bleak vocal line that scarcely moves for eight long measures. Proudly he then asserts his triumph—"Victor and vanquished alike I subdue." No solace is offered the poor victims, for they will be forgotten by all except by Death, who will tramp down the earth over their graves so that they may never rise again.

In direct contrast to these grim songs are the many satiric and comic works by this composer. A group of songs written in 1866–67 to his own texts, including "Darling Savishna," "You Drunken Sot," and "The Seminarist," shows his strong ironic bent: in the first the village idiot babbles of his love to the local beauty, in the second a woman scolds her drunken spouse, in the third a theology student tries to memorize Latin nouns while erotic thoughts about his mentor's luscious daughter torment him. The most famous of Moussorgsky's comic songs is his last (1879), "The Flea," from Goethe's *Faust* (in Russian translation). The cynical "ha ha ha ha ha," sung to the first five notes of a minor scale, mock the pomposity of the Flea, dressed in silks and velvets, and the vanity and idiocy of self-important people.

Musical caricatures such as "The Classicist," which pokes fun at a critic who disliked Rimsky-Korsakov's opera *Sadko* because of its avant-garde ideas, are realistic and delightfully malicious. The critic's protestations of artistic purity are set to banal, insipid music, with the most carefully correct final V–I cadence on record!

A group of songs to texts by A. K. Tolstoy (1877) employs what Moussorgsky called "intelligently justified melody," a combination of melody and declamation. Among these songs are "Pride," "Shall a Man Spin?" and "Softly the Spirit Flew Up to Heaven." In these works Moussorgsky stresses once again his conviction that music must be a form of communication, that art for art's sake is wrong, that truth takes precedence over beauty and indeed is beauty.

Borodin and Moussorgsky belonged to a little coterie of nationalistic composers loosely organized around Mily Alexeyevich Balakirev (1837–1910); the group also included César Antonovitch Cui (1835–1918) and Nikolai Rimsky-Korsakov (1844–1908). Sometimes referred to as "The Five" outside of Russia, they were always known as "the mighty handful" in their own land. They did much to realize their mutual goal of creating a national style by joining Russia's musical heritage to her distinctive literary genius. Since this style is predicated on a naturalistic setting of the language, few of the songs of these composers are known to us in translation; since few European or American singers are familiar with even the Russian alphabet much less the language, one encounters these marvelously evocative songs far less often than might be expected.

Conspicuous by his absence from the above-mentioned group is Peter Ilich Tchaikovsky (1840–1893), one of the few "serious" composers to achieve and sustain enormous popularity with the non-concert-going masses. Tchaikovsky never fully subscribed to the nationalistic aims of the "mighty handful." Feeling that the music of Mozart and the Italian masters was as much a part of his personal heritage as the Russian folk music he also loved, he attempted to fuse these elements by adding folk-coloristic touches to his basically cosmopolitan style. This may also be said of Sergei Rachmaninov (1873–1943), an equally popular composer of the next generation.

If one were to judge Tchaikovsky's output only by his songs, the above statement would seem highly questionable, for the Russian element often looms large in his hundred or so works in this genre. The melancholia, despairing passion, and bittersweet sentiment which lie at the heart of most Russian music are found in the majority of his songs. When the texts are by Russian poets, as is most often the case, Tchaikovsky's identification with his native land seems strong indeed. Nevertheless, the Italianate melodies, lush cantilenas, and virtuosic vocal climaxes of so many of his songs often distort the texts, destroying the naturalistic relationship between words and music which underlies the Russian national style. Obviously the declamatory, parlando vocal line was anathema to a man of Tchaikovsky's temperament.

Among Tchaikovsky's finest songs are the seven of Opus 47 (1880). All the texts are Russian, four by A. K. Tolstoy. In the first, "Had I Only Known," balalaika-like chords introduce a folklike melody, which features a falling interval of a fourth. The accompanying figure is a monotonous drone. Suddenly the folk lament yields to a graceful waltz, as the protagonist imagines a ballroom scene. The climax of the song is a cry of pain, after which the music of the opening section returns. The quasi-operatic song represents not so much a fusion as a juxtaposition of native and European music.

"Does the Day Dawn?" Opus 47 No. 6 (text by Apukhtin), begins with a very long, elaborate piano prelude. In fact, as often happens in Tchaikovsky's songs, the piano part tends to overwhelm the vocal line. The free, impassioned melody has few obviously "Russian" touches. The final song of the set, "Was I Not a Blade of Grass?" whose text is a

Russian translation by Surikov of a Ukrainian poem by Shevchenko, has an equally elaborate piano part, but its melody is more manifestly Russian, especially in the virtuosic cadenzas. Both of these songs are passionate outcries.

In his last song, "Again, as Before, Alone" (1893, text by Rathaus), heavy chords in the piano part emphasize the painfully intense emotions of melody and text. In a lighter vein are the *Sixteen Songs for Children* of Opus 54, but nowhere is the sardonic wit of Borodin or Moussorgsky in evidence.

Although most of his compositions are little more than salon pieces, mention must be made of Anton Rubinstein, (1830–1894) whose *Persian Songs*, Opus 34, were extremely popular during his lifetime. During the 1940s his setting of Pushkin's beautiful love poem, "Night," was exploited as an American popular ballad under the title "If You Are But a Dream." Another composer of attractive albeit less important songs was Alexander Glazunov (1865–1936) who emphasized the Eastern aspects of Russian music in such songs as "Oriental Romance" (text by Pushkin).

Best known of the turn-of-the-century Russians was Sergei Rachmaninov who lived until 1943. Although a contemporary of such modernists as Schoenberg and Stravinsky, his post-Romantic style, with its sentimental tunes and lush harmonies, places his music squarely in the nineteenth century. The heart-on-the-sleeve emotions of so many of his songs strike responsive chords in vast numbers of listeners, and it is impossible to deny the beauty of melodies like the one given primarily to the piano in "Oh, Never Sing to Me Again" (Opus 4 No. 4, text by Pushkin). Since Rachmaninov was a brilliant pianist who wrote well for the keyboard— his piano preludes and concerti, among which one must include his *Variations on a Theme by Paganini*, are his most popular works—it is not surprising that the piano parts for his songs are rich and often virtuosic. In "Oh, Never Sing to Me Again," the text refers to "that haunting melody" which recalls the memory of the lost loved one. Although the vocal line is also lyrical and lovely, it is clearly the piano's tune that haunts the poet.

Opus 4, one of seven sets of songs composed by Rachmaninov between 1890 and 1916, contains several other very appealing songs, including the first of the group, "Please Don't Go," which has a wistful, pleading melody, the third, "In the Silence of the Night," with its particularly beautiful piano part, and the fifth, "The Harvest of Sorrow," the most obviously "Russian" of those mentioned. There is a glorious vocal cadenza on the final "Ah" of this last song.

Other Rachmaninov favorites are "Lilacs" from Opus 21, "Oh, Do Not Grieve" from Opus 14, and "The Storm" from Opus 34, all of which feature romantic vocal lines and sonorous piano parts. There is no attempt on Rachmaninov's part to be innovative in these songs, and yet they all bear the stamp of his musical personality.

In a more contemplative vein we find "To the Children" (Opus 26 No. 7, text by Khomyakov), a quiet song completely devoid of pyrotechnics, which bemoans the emptiness of the paternal home after the children have gone. Religious sentiment is expressed in the final verse (the accompaniment has churchlike chords) when the father asks for his children's prayers. "Christ Is Risen," from the same opus (text by Merezhkovsky) is a very Russian-sounding lament in which the poet says that Christ would shed bitter tears if he could see "how base is man."

Opus 34, a group of fourteen songs (1912), concludes with "Vocalise," probably the best-known wordless song in the repertoire. Its gorgeous melody has been borrowed by

violinists, violists, and cellists, its lovely contours well-suited
to the pulsating vibrato of a string instrument.

Despite her late start in the area of serious music, and in
the face of political upheavals and subsequent oppression of
artistic freedom, Russia has produced three of the key figures
in music of the first half of the twentieth century: Igor Stravinsky (1882–1971), Sergei Prokofiev (1891–1953), and
Dimitri Shostakovich (1906–1975). None of these highly individualistic and innovative composers concentrated his
powers on solo songs, but Shostakovich's thirteenth and
fourteenth symphonies, Mahlerian symphonic song cycles,
are among his greatest achievements.

Stravinsky's great contribution to Russian nationalism
was, paradoxically, his cosmopolitan outlook, for he redi-
verted the Russian spirit, strengthened by its nineteenth-
century self-absorption, to the international scene, thereby
saving it from ingrown parochialism. Russian composers
were now secure enough to retain their individuality while
joining the mainstream.

Like Stravinsky, Prokofiev lived for a while in Paris,
cultivating Gallic wit in the style of Poulenc and others of
"Les Six." In most of his later works this sophisticated
tongue in cheekiness became mordant satire, but in his songs
he retains a good-natured charm and humor. His Opus 18,
The Ugly Duckling (1914), is a long narrative song in which
the piano aids in the storytelling. There is so much humor
in the music that one needn't understand the text to be forced
to chuckle. His five *Poems by Anna Akhmatova* (Opus
27, 1916) are brief lyric sketches ranging in mood from
tenderness to gentle melancholia. Only in the last does
one hear traces of bleak sorrow. The *Five Songs Without
Words* (Opus 35, 1920–25) and *Three Romances* (Opus 73,

1936, poems by Pushkin) are again lyric and romantic, only occasionally spiced by "wrong-note" chords and quirky rhythms. On the whole Prokofiev's songs are remarkably conservative, and while quite pleasant in themselves, they do not really represent the composer's strength and originality.

The career of Dimitri Shostakovich presents an enigma to the Free World: alternately hailed and assailed by Soviet authorities, his compositions range from docile, facile propaganda to brilliant, defiant masterworks. In the latter category we find Symphonies 13 and 14, fairly recent works (1962 and 1969 respectively) which caused their composer much travail. Number 13, entitled *Babi Yar*, is as much a cantata as a symphony. It employs a tremendous orchestra (many extra woodwinds, brass, and percussion), male soloist, and male chorus. Its five poems, all by Yevtushenko, criticize aspects of Russian society. The first, from which the work gets its name, is a heartrending denunciation of anti-Semitism. The soloist sings "It seems to me that now I am a Jew/ And now I am on a cross, crucified, dying." Recalling Dreyfus, Anne Frank, and victims of pogroms, the poet berates those who harass Jews, saying that he, as much hated by anti-Semites as the Jews are, is a true Russian (this powerful last line is sung by soloist and chorus).

The other poems deal in turn with "Humor," which no repressive forces can kill, women waiting in line "At the Store"—a very serious theme treated dramatically and in deadly earnest—"Fears," and "A Career." Themes of collective and individual responsibility (never dissimulate to advance your career—to your own self be true) run through the poems.

Shostakovich's setting is massive. The soloist bears most of the narrative burden, the chorus either echoing or commenting on his words, often in plainsong unison. The

orchestra provides graphic illustration (heavy-booted marching when the Nazis come to take Anne Frank, a sardonic
fiddle solo in "Humor," onomatopoeic clicks to represent
"the clatter of cans" in "At the Store," and so forth), and
atmospheric effects (the strange, ominous tuba solo at the
beginning of "Fears," for instance).

Even more effective is the Fourteenth Symphony, an
eleven-poem cycle to texts by Garcia Lorca, Apollinaire,
Rilke, and a little-known Russian contemporary of Pushkin
named Küchelbecker. Each of these poems—all used in Russian translation—deals with death, but the enormous variety
in Shostakovich's music prevents monotony. The scoring is
for strings, an extensive percussion section, soprano, and
baritone.

The first song, "De Profundis" (Lorca) deals with the
tragic death of lovers. The baritone sings the bleak declamatory lines, which sound like a requiem by Moussorgsky. In
contrast, the second song, sung by soprano, "Malaguena"
(Lorca), is a macabre little scherzo. Country fiddles and castanets strike up a bitter waltz as Death visits a Spanish
tavern. The third song, a duet, "Lorelei" (Apollinaire), features galloping horses, xylophone, gongs, and bells. A gentle
refrain, "Tri lilii, tri lilii, lilii tri na mogile mayei bez leresta"
("Three lilies, three lilies, lilies three on my grave without a
cross") is heard throughout the fourth song, "The Suicide,"
in which soprano and solo cello sing a poignant duet.

"On Watch," for soprano (Apollinaire), is a sardonic
parody of military music, featuring xylophone, wood blocks,
and drums. The woman's bizarre words explain that she
wants to look beautiful "In incest and death" for her brother-
lover who must be killed in battle. In "Madam, Look!" a
duet, the onomatopoeic Russian word for laugh, "khokho-
chou" (almost "ho ho ho"), is used in bitter irony, as the
woman laughs at "love which is cut down by death."

The longest of the sections is the seventh, "The Prison" (bass, Apollinaire). Unusually extensive orchestral interludes, in which the strings play pizzicato (plucked) or col legno (the wood of the bow hitting the strings), depict the hapless prisoner pacing back and forth in his cell. This and the ninth song are the strongest political statements in the symphony.

In the eighth song, also by Apollinaire and again for bass, cossacks hurl insults at the sultan. The ninth, "O Delvig, Delvig" (Küchelbecker), is an affirmation of faith in "bold inspired deeds and sweet song" despite imprisonment and death. The penultimate song, "Death of the Poet" (Rilke), begins with an echo of the music of the symphony's introductory passage for high strings, this time in duet with the soprano. The conclusion, again by Rilke, unites the two singers for a final elegy to Death, the all powerful, who weeps within us.

This extraordinary symphonic song cycle, with its exotic orchestral effects, its alternation between orchestral tuttis and solo instruments alone and in combination with the voices, its masterful setting of poems of four nations, is a brilliant combination of the intensely Russian spirit and universal, eternal truths.

Nationalism, Part II: Spain, Norway, Bohemia, Finland, and Denmark

During the Middle Ages and early Renaissance, Spain was as musically active as any other European area. The stultifying effects of the Inquisition, with the concomitant expulsion of the Jews and Moors, eventually served to dry up creative originality in all the arts, and during the seventeenth, eighteenth, and nineteenth centuries Spanish composers were very much eclipsed by the Germans, French, and Italians. Folk music alone flourished during this long fallow period, which saw the development of the zarzuela, a music drama with song, dance, and spoken dialogue and the tonadilla, a sort of miniature comic opera which fused folk and composed popular music. Aside from these popular lightweight musical entertainments, there were only imitations or importations of Italian and French opera and operetta.

In the last quarter of the nineteenth century Felipe Pedrell (1841–1922), a highly respected composer and teacher, urged young Spaniards to explore their native musical heritage as a way of revitalizing the moribund Spanish tradition of serious music. The Spanish idiom had already attracted attention via the works of French composers such as Bizet, Lalo, Chabrier, and Debussy. Even the Russian composers Glinka and Rimsky-Korsakov had exploited Spanish dance rhythms and instrumentation (guitar, tambourine, and castanets), the former in his *Spanish Overtures* of 1845 and 1848, the latter in his *Capriccio Espagnol* of 1887. Now it was time for some Spanish music by Spanish composers.

Three important composers emerged from this nationalistic movement—Enrique Granados (1867–1916), Isaac Albéniz (1860–1909), and Manuel de Falla (1876–1946)—but their total contribution to the song literature is quite small, Albéniz adding almost nothing of interest.

Aside from a few youthful efforts, Granados's entire song catalog consists of the seven *Canciones Amatorias* (*Love Songs*) and the ten *Tonadillas al Estilo Antiguo* (*Tonadillas in Antique Style*). Most of the *Love Songs* are lyrical and tender. Their extremely subtle Spanish flavor is balanced by Granados's cosmopolitan style, although the influence of folk song is quite apparent in "No Llorcis, Ojuelos," the fifth of the set. The gentle melancholia which pervades the songs is far removed from the heavy sorrow of much folk-inspired Russian music.

Granados's two greatest works, the suite of six piano pieces called *Goyescas* and the ten tonadillas, were both inspired by the composer's admiration for the paintings of Francisco Goya (1746–1828), one of Spain's greatest artists. Granados attempted to evoke the style of music found in the tonadillas (comic operettas) of Goya's day by using archaic harmonies and accompaniments suggestive of folk instrumentation—primarily guitar. His title is somewhat misleading, for technically these are not tonadillas at all, just individual songs.

Like many of Goya's paintings, Granados's tonadillas are portraits of "Majas" and "Majos"—women and men of Madrid. The set opens with a triptych, "La Maja Dolorosa" Nos. 1, 2, and 3, a sad woman's three-part lament over the death of her lover. The three songs are thematically interrelated, and the final portrait, "La Maja de Goya," brings back their lovely melodies. "El Tra la la y el Punteado," the fourth song of the set, is based on lively dance rhythms. Its "tra la la la la" refrain is echoed by the guitar. The following song, "El Mirar de la Maja," is melancholy, but the sixth, "Callijeo," is gay and flirtatious. The mood alternates once again from the poignant "Amor y Odio" to the bright charm of the last three sketches, "El Majo Discreto," "El Majo Timido," and "La Maja de Goya." Aside from the first three songs, the tonadillas do not dwell on the darker side of Goya's genius, nor do we find any trace of the macabre or grotesque, which characterizes so many of his paintings.

De Falla wrote even fewer songs than Granados: the *Trois Mélodies* to poems by French poet Théophile Gautier (1909), the vocal movements of the ballet *El Amor Brujo*

(1915), and the *Seven Spanish Popular Songs* (1922). These last are extremely skillful transformations of folk songs, including the famous "Jota" (No. 4) which has been transcribed for violin and piano. Throughout the set the piano imitates the guitar, often with virtuosic brilliance. Dance rhythms abound, not only in the "Jota" but in the "Segudilla murciana" (No. 2) and the "Polo" (No. 7), which has a wild, flamenco-like accompaniment. The third, fifth, and sixth songs ("Asturiana," "Nana," and "Canción") are dark and brooding. "Nana" is especially tender and beautiful.

Slightly younger than this illustrious triumvirate was Joaquín Turina (1882–1949), a most successful and effective composer of songs. Turina and Manuel de Falla, living in Paris at about the same time, were subjected to the same influences, primarily the music of French composers d'Indy, Debussy, and Ravel. Nevertheless, under the guidance of Albéniz, who also lived in the French capital, both younger composers continued to emphasize the elements of Spanish folk music which characterize their styles.

Turina's love for the piano is evident in all his song settings, especially in the cycle *Poema en forma de canciones* (texts by R. de Campoamor) and the *Dos canciones* of Opus 38 (texts by Cristina de Arteaga), both of which begin with long sections for piano solo. The cycle, an early work (1919, Opus 19), features a delicate "Dedication," in which the pianist lovingly and gently sets the mood for the four love poems which follow. Tenderness pervades the music, but Spanish impetuosity creeps into the final song ("Las Locas por amor") in which the Goddess Venus says she—like all women—prefers to be loved briefly but madly, rather than forever in moderation!

Turina's vocal catalog consists of two dozen songs for voice and piano, one of which is a wordless "Vocalizaciones"

(Opus 74, 1932), and a seven-song cycle for voice and orchestra (*Canto a Sevilla*, Opus 37, 1927).

A lesser-known composer, Joaquín Rodrigo (b. 1902), has written a handful of attractive songs, including four *Madrigales Amatorios* and *Canciones sobre textos castillanos* (*Songs to Castilian words*). The first two madrigals feature antique-sounding final cadences (especially the first) and wistful, yearning melodies; in contrast the third and fourth are gay, humorous folk tunes with coloraturo vocal lines.

In the 1940s a musical comedy based on the life and music of Edvard Grieg (1843–1907) appeared on Broadway under the title *Song of Norway*. No name could have been more apt, for Grieg's music is indeed the voice of his native land.

Grieg was a fine melodist, very much in the style of Schumann, and nowhere is he as inspired as in his 150-odd songs. His peculiar harmonic trademark, the progression from a minor triad to a major chord based on the raised seventh of the first (an F minor to an E major, for instance), seems to evoke the Norwegian landscape without reference to actual folk music. Grieg often uses a raised seventh over a minor chord melodically as well, as, for instance, in his beautiful song "Hidden Love" (Opus 39 No. 2) in which the second bar of the essentially B minor melody has an A sharp over the B minor accompanying chords. This suggests the same open-air freshness.

Grieg's most famous song is undoubtedly "I Love You" (Opus 5 No. 3). Its touchingly simple melody is beautifully suited to the heartfelt declaration of love by Hans Christian Andersen (1805–1875) which comprises its text. It is too early a piece to be characteristic of the mature composer, but it deserves its fame nevertheless. Also to a text by Andersen is the frolicsome "Woodland Wandering" (Opus 18 No. 1) which depicts a breezy forest glade on a warm summer night, but is transformed into a song about Christmas in *Song of Norway*. Also used in the Broadway score were the hauntingly beautiful "Springtime" (Opus 33 No. 2) and "With a Water Lily" (Opus 25 No. 4). The latter has a text by Henrik Ibsen.

Although some of Grieg's songs fail to rise above the level of salon music, a surprising number are very effective. To those already mentioned we should add "Ragnheld" (Opus 44 No. 3), "The Princess" (Opus 21 No. 4), and "Radiant Night" (Opus 70 No. 3), all of which exemplify Grieg's harmonic patterns, and "At the Bier of a Young Woman" (Opus 39 No. 5) which features a lovely duet between voice and piano.

Most listeners delight in the ethnically oriented music of the area once known as Bohemia, its colorful Magyar, Moravian, and Slovakian elements bringing exotic flavor to its Germanic underpinnings. The most creative composers from this part of the world were Czechoslovakians Bedřich Smetana (1824–1884), Antonín Dvořák (1841–1904), and Leoš Janáček (1850–1928), and Hungarians Béla Bartók (1881–1945), and Zoltán Kodály (1882–1967).

Although Janáček, Bartók, and Kodály wrote settings for dozens of folk songs, seeking the most authentic harmonies and rhythms by serious study of the music of indigenous peoples, of the above-named composers only Dvořák created a large body of original solo and duo songs (about a hundred). The few examples of composed songs by Bartók, Kodály and Janáček that do exist are so wedded to the Hungarian and Slovakian languages that translations are rarely successful; nevertheless few singers of international renown choose to learn these extremely difficult tongues. We have already encountered this problem in Russian songs, and shall meet it again in the songs of Sibelius, whose texts are usually Swedish or Finnish, and Nielsen, who sets mostly Danish poems.

Dvořák's most popular song, one that is often heard in terribly insipid English translation, is "Songs My Mother Taught Me," the fourth of seven *Gypsy Songs,* Opus 55, to texts of Adolf Heyduk. Even if one can swallow the "measure / treasure" rhymes, the tune itself is too sentimental to typify this often inspired composer. Of higher quality, although still far from top-drawer Dvořák, is "The Maiden's Lament," Opus 73 No. 3, one of four Czech folk poems, also usually sung in English in the United States. In this song one can hear touches of Dvořák's characteristic harmonic progressions, especially toward the end. Although critics usually cite Dvořák's *Biblical Songs* (Opus 99) as his best vocal works, his personal favorites appear to have been the four songs from Opus 82, especially "Leave Me Alone," the first of the group. These are settings of German poems by Ottilie Malybrok-Stieler, a mediocre German poet who had great empathy for Czech culture. While pleasant enough, they do not rise to the excellence of Dvořák's instrumental works. The last, "At the Brook," uses a Schubertian figure to portray the running water, but its vocal line lacks Schubert's inspired touch. More appealing are the *Moravian Duets,* Opus 32, thirteen settings of Moravian folk poems for soprano, contralto, and piano (1876), which often capture the lilt and abandon of folk song and dance. The sixth, "The Forsaken Lassie," is especially charming.

Although Janáček's most important works are vocal—his opera *Jenufa* and his enormous Slavonic Mass are superb examples—he wrote few solo songs. *The Diary of One Who Vanished* (1916–19), a twenty-two-part cycle for tenor, contralto, chorus of three female voices, and piano, is his major effort in the genre. Its text, brief poems written by a peasant lad and left behind as an explanation of his disappearance, recounts how he met a beautiful gypsy girl, was seduced by her, fathered her son, and left home to travel with her. He is full of remorse toward his beloved parents and sister, ashamed of his sin, and degraded by the nomadic life he will now lead.

The cycle's format is unusual: the tenor sings the first eight parts alone; the ninth song is a dialogue between the gypsy and the lad, upon which the chorus comments; the tenth is a long solo for the contralto, again with comments from the chorus. Aside from the thirteenth, a piano solo, the tenor sings all the other sections.

For the most part the melodic style of the *Diary* seems to be a natural outgrowth of Janáček's studies of speech rhythms and inflections. The vocal line always advances the story without melismatic embellishment. The piano part is conservative when compared to Bartók's exactly contemporary Opus 16 songs (see below), as it is clearly diatonic and not unduly dissonant. In one small section, the twentieth, voice and music aid the irony of the words ("I have a damsel, may she be praised / The skirt around her waist is oh, so highly raised"). On the whole the work is most effective.

Of all the ethnic composers, none were more directly influenced by folk music than Béla Bartók and Zoltán Kodály, who worked together collecting and recording genuine folk songs and dances of Magyar and other sects in Bulgaria, Rumania, and Hungary. Their research led to their notating incredibly complex rhythmic patterns hitherto ignored by other nationalistic composers; in some cases measures are divided into uneven combinations of eighth notes, such as:

$$\frac{4+2+3}{8} \text{ or } \frac{3+3+2}{8}$$

Their folk-song settings are lovely, unhackneyed, and have the undeniable aura of authenticity.

Of their composed songs, the outstanding work is Bartók's Opus 16 (1916), five songs to poems of the Hungarian poet Endre Ady. The morose texts deal with autumn and death, and the vocal lines are bleak and declamatory. Occasionally the piano part is subtly descriptive—the introductory chords and arpeggios in "The Sound of Autumn" (No. 2) which suggest the fog on an autumn night, the vaguely watery arpeggios in "Alone with the Sea" (No. 4)—but on the whole there is little atmospheric variety from one song to the next. Most expressive of the set is the third, "My Bed Is Calling," in which the anguish of the words can be felt in the strong chords and soaring vocal line. In these songs the melodic rhythms are too closely related to the accents peculiar to the Hungarian language for translations to be feasible.

Kodály's best-known composed songs are the five of Opus 9 (1915–18), two of which have texts by Ady and three by Béla Balzs. Although "Sappho's Love Song," the first of the set, is somewhat more lyrically romantic than the others, the overall mood is bleak and mysterious. In "The Forest," one of the Balzs texts, the words and music of an old folk-song are quoted. Aside from this interpolation the songs are not obviously folk-derived.

Far more lushly romantic are the songs of Finnish composer Jean Sibelius (1865–1957). Although deeply imbued with the spirit of Finnish folk music, Sibelius often preferred to set poetry in Swedish, a language taught in the public schools and thought of as part of Finland's cultural heritage.

Several of Sibelius's songs, including the dramatic "Black Roses" (Opus 36 No. 1, text by Ernst Josephson), are well-known in English translation, but many others from Sibelius's almost hundred-song catalog, while equally lovely, are unfamiliar to American audiences.

In general the songs are richly melodic. Since Sibelius makes no attempt to be "modern," the accompaniments seem conservative without being derivative. Throughout songs with such disparate subjects as "The First Kiss" (Opus 72 No. 3), "On a Balcony by the Sea" (Opus 38 No. 2), and "The Tryst" (Opus 37 No. 5), there runs a thread of heartbreak and gloom, as though the melancholia of Finland's long winter's sunless days cannot be shaken. "Spring Flies Fast" (Opus 13 No. 4) is unusually gay for Sibelius, but "Come Away, Death" (Opus 60 No. 1), a Swedish translation of a Shakespearean text set for either piano or guitar (it would be accompanied by a lute in the original play), is appropriately sorrowful. Particularly poignant is a little passage where the accompaniment rises to the words "Fly away, fly away, breath" only to be squelched by the vocal line. The soft sibilant sound of the words "Säf, säf, susa" ("Sigh, rushes, sigh"), set to high tremolos in the accompaniment, makes this a particularly lovely song.

Sibelius's Danish contemporary, Carl Nielsen (1865–1931) developed a totally different style in his attempt to establish a Danish national school, composing very simple piano accompaniments which double the folk-derived vocal lines of his charmingly naive songs. He wanted Danish schoolchildren to be able to sing his songs, thus cultivating their love of music, and to a very large extent his aims have been realized.

Contemporary England and the U.S.A.

The late nineteenth-century revitalization of England's musical life is largely attributable to the sudden interest in English folk music sparked by the efforts of Cecil Sharp (1859–1924), the rediscovery of the music of the Tudor period, and a renewed interest in the works of Henry Purcell.

Frederick Delius (1862–1934) and Sir Edward Elgar (1857–1934) were the founding fathers of the new English school. Of the two Delius was the more gifted songwriter, while Elgar's rather rhetorical style was better suited to oratorio. Delius, totally alienated from the bourgeois milieu into which he was born, traveled widely. He set French and German poetry as well as English and German translations of Swedish and Norwegian texts, thus underscoring the eclectic nature of his music. In a way his style is an exaggerated amalgamation of European trends, relying more heavily than the French Impressionists on the vague augmented chord, modulating more doggedly than Wagner. The influence of Grieg, a composer he much admired, may be heard in several of his songs, particularly the lovely "The Homeward Way," one of twelve *Songs from the Norwegian* he dedicated to Grieg's wife. Despite all these influences Delius's works bear the stamp of his own peculiar temperament and style; in absorbing and personalizing diffuse elements, he produced original, essentially nonderivative music.

Among Delius's more successful songs are the *Three Verlaine Songs*: "Il Pleure dans mon coeur," "Le Ciel est, Par-dessus la Toit," and "La Lune Blanche." The haunting words of these three well-known texts are well served by Delius's vague harmonies and atmospheric sounds. In the first of the set Delius uses the repeated-note declamatory vocal line so characteristic of Debussy. The oft-heard countermelody in the piano part suggests languor and ennui. Despite its charm, however, the setting of the second song trivializes the powerful text, first by giving a happy little song for the bird to sing, and second by repeating the last phrase, "de ta jeunesse," to the bird-song figure. In all three songs the settings by Fauré and Debussy are much stronger and more appropriate.

Delius's most important vocal work—indeed one of his best efforts in any genre—is generally thought to be "Sea Drift," for baritone, chorus, and orchestra. In this work (1903) which uses poems of Walt Whitman, Delius expresses his pantheistic love of nature. Chorus and orchestra— particularly the harp—swell and ebb like the vast sea. Sensual harmonies and constant modulations suggest the ever-changing contours of the undulating waters. The voices blend with the orchestra—indeed they become part of the orchestral texture. Periodically the solo baritone stands apart, carefully enunciating the words with their painstakingly accurate syllabification. Only in the songs of Sibelius do we hear this kind of prosody, in which each syllable is given equal time.

Of Elgar's many choral works, the most highly regarded is *The Dream of Gerontius,* an ambitious oratorio for three solo voices, chorus, and orchestra, based on a text which is a profound personal expression of religious faith by John Henry Cardinal Newman. In this massive work Elgar fuses the Händelian oratorio format to the post-Wagnerian style of vocal and orchestral writing. The setting of the English words (there are occasional references in Latin to sections of the Mass) is in complete accord with natural speech rhythms, and there are few deliberately archaic devices other than the use of modal plainsong in such choral passages as "Rescue him, O Lord, in this his evil hour . . ."

More directly influenced by the folk-music revival than either Delius or Elgar was Ralph Vaughan Williams who, with his contemporary and friend Gustav Holst, moved English music closer to its own origins and further from German, French, and Italian hegemony. It is impossible to determine whether his love for old English music or his own English-country-gentleman personality was the more responsible for the decidedly nationalistic nature of Vaughan Williams's music, but an English flavor certainly does pervade his compositions. This is especially apparent in his many songs, for which he used traditional texts or poems by English poets Robert Louis Stevenson, Alfred, Lord Tennyson, the Rossettis, Coleridge, A. E. Housman, and Shakespeare.

Although many of Vaughan Williams's best-known vocal pieces are folk-song settings (it was his setting of "Greensleeves" that revived its popularity), we shall discuss only his original songs. The difference is often hard to discern, especially in strophic songs such as "Linden Lea" (ca. 1900, words by W. Barnes) which are enough like folk music to belie their composed status. More obviously original are the two sets of *Songs of Travel* to poems by R. L. Stevenson. These are songs of youth, of love, of unexplored worlds to conquer, of yearning, and of tenderness. In "Let Beauty Awake," the first song of the second set, the accompaniment has rich, full arpeggiated chords to support the manly, vigorous vocal part. The next song, "Youth and Love," conveys a sense of wonderment at the glories of earth and sky. Its accompaniment alternately divides the quarter note into regular eighth notes and triplet eighth notes; its melodic line is sometimes declamatory and sometimes rhapsodic. After a tremendous climax, Vaughan Williams gives us a beautiful modulation and a sudden pianissimo for the words "Sings but a boyish stave." The last two songs of the group are quiet and lovely.

The *Five Mystical Songs* of 1911 to words by George Herbert testify to Vaughan Williams's deep religious feelings. Ideally performed by baritone, chorus, and orchestra, they can also be done by solo singer with piano accompaniment. In these songs we hear many modal passages, with particularly effective use of the whole step between the seventh note of the scale and the octave (see the final two measures of the opening melody in the second song, "I Got Me Flowers," for instance). There is complete rhythmic freedom, 3/4 measures followed by 2/4 or 4/4 according to the demands of the texts. As was commonly done in Purcell's day, key words are often extended over several notes for emphasis: in "The Call," for example, the first syllable of the word "killeth" ("Life, as killeth death") is given a melismatic line of seven notes. "Antiphon," the last of the *Mystical Songs,* has the wonderfully clangorous sound of antiphonal bells or brass even in its piano reduction. On the whole this group is poignant and beautiful. It combines the folk, antique, and original aspects of Vaughan William's most representative compositions.

Another highly regarded cycle by Vaughan Williams consists of six settings of poems by A. E. Housman for tenor, string quartet, and piano. Known by the title of its first poem, *On Wenlock Edge,* its poems deal with death and loss of love. Perhaps the most touching of the set is "Is My Team Ploughing?" (the third) in which the dead youth queries his best friend, only to find that life goes on without him—even his beloved is content in her new love for the friend. "Oh, When I Was in Love with You," which follows, has a folklike tune, but Vaughan Williams provides sophisticated touches in the accompaniment. "Bredon Hall" is equally folklike and features onomatopoeic pealing bells in the accompaniment. There are many descriptive passages in the music, especially in the first song where we are made to hear the wind running riot through the woods.

Gustav Holst owes more to the Tudor tradition than to folk song per se. In his beautiful songs for voice and violin (Opus 35, 1916), four medieval lyrics are set to modal, plain-song-like melodies. "I Sing of a Maiden," the most effective of this very fine set, begins with unaccompanied voice; when the violin joins the voice after the first two lines of verse, the two melodies are interwoven with great delicacy and beauty.

In much the same style are *Six Medieval Lyrics* of 1932 for chorus of men's voices and strings. In this group, of which the fourth and fifth ("Intercession" and "Good Friday") are outstanding, polytonality is combined with modal chant and antique cadences. Holst also wrote many unaccompanied canons for chorus or two or more solo singers.

The outstanding twentieth-century English composer of vocal music to date is undoubtedly Benjamin Britten. His operas which include *Peter Grimes, Billy Budd, Prodigal Son,* and *Death in Venice,* his choral works, his cycles for solo voice and orchestra, and those for solo voice and piano are favorites with audiences and performers alike. Although

thoroughly British in his acknowledged indebtedness to folk
song and Henry Purcell, Britten successfully set French
Symbolist Rimbaud's difficult *Les Illuminations* (Opus 18,
1939) and *Seven Sonnets of Michelangelo* (Opus 22, 1940) in
their original languages. More accessible are his charming
folk-song settings, volume I in English (this includes the
delightfully comic "Oliver Cromwell Is Buried and Dead"
which ends with the sassy "If you want any more you can
sing it yourself" and has therefore become a favorite last
encore!), the second volume in French, and the third once
again in English. "Sally Gardens" and "The Ash Grove,"
both from volume I of the Folksong Arrangements, are particularly lovely examples of Britten's ability to combine simplicity and sophistication, making the settings appropriate to
the folk idiom but original and arresting at the same time.

Although *Grove's Dictionary* calls him "one of diatonicism's best living advertisements" (unfortunately he is no
longer alive, having died in 1976), Britten often looked back
to modal plainsong (*The Prodigal Son*) and forward to new
harmonic combinations (*Songs and Proverbs of William
Blake,* 1965). Two of his most important cycles—he wrote
few single songs, usually preferring interrelated sets of texts
—are *The Holy Sonnets of John Donne,* 1945, and the Blake
Proverbs and Songs. The Donne Sonnets (Opus 35) open
with a dramatic setting of "Oh, My Blacke Soule," in which
the piano has forceful dotted-rhythm unisons while the voice
intones with passion. The mood and sound are bleak. Sudden excitement comes with "Batter My Heart"; sorrowful
pleading and repentance follow with "Oh, Might These
Sighs and Tears." In "Oh, to Vex Me" the voice recites the
words at the breakneck speed of a Gilbert and Sullivan patter
song, a style often used by Britten but unexpected in this
very serious group. The penultimate song of the set, "Thou
Hast Made Me," also calls for rapid-fire delivery of the

words. The seventh and ninth (last) songs, "At the Round Earth's Imagined Corners" and "Death Be Not Proud," are the most obviously Elizabethan. The former begins with a rousing fanfare and ends with unaccompanied plainsong; the latter is a solemn march with Händelian double-dotted rhythms and Purcellian multinote syllables.

The *Songs and Proverbs of William Blake* resembles Beethoven's cycle *An die ferne Geliebte* in that individual units cannot stand alone, a characteristic piano figure linking one to the next. Britten has arranged Blake's texts so that there are indispensable links in the words as well, the proverb about friendship ("The bird a nest, the spider a web, man friendship") leading into "A Poison Tree" which begins "I was angry with my friend," "Tyger, Tyger, Burning Bright" followed by the proverb "The tygers of wrath are wiser than the horses of instruction," and so forth.

In this cycle we hear Britten's most advanced harmonic ideas, polytonality and atonality happily coexisting with diatonicism. The proverbs are solemnly intoned while the songs are given full dramatic treatment. Sometimes the mood of the music seems at odds with the words of the proverbs—"Think in the morning. Act in the noon. Eat in the evening" sounds ominous and foreboding; "The bird a nest . . . " is vaguely mysterious—but the longer songs are musically expressive of their narrative content. Despite the cynicism of some of the earlier selections (proverb II: "Prisons are built with stones of Law / Brothels with bricks of Religion"), the cycle ends optimistically, with the lovely "To See a World in a Grain of Sand" as the last proverb, "Every Night and Every Morn" for the last song, and an affirmation of tonality in the final measures of music.

The first Americans to achieve more than local renown in art song were Edward MacDowell (1861–1908) and

Charles Griffes (1884–1920), both of whom based their compositions on European traditions.

Far more American in sound than the works of Mac-Dowell or Griffes are the songs of Charles Ives (1874–1954). Composing primarily for his own satisfaction, refusing to publicize or even publish his works, this rugged individualist anticipated just about every twentieth-century innovation—polytonality, polyrhythms, atonality, free dissonant counterpoint, tone clusters, and so on. One would call his works seminal but for the fact that they were known to too few musicians to influence the mainstream of music until long after similar ideas had appeared independently in the works of others.

Most of Ives's instrumental works still seem difficult and inaccessible to the average listener, although such pieces as the "Turkey in the Straw" movement of the Second Violin Sonata or the patriotic marches at the end of the Second Symphony should be fun for anyone to hear. The best introduction to Ives's music is undoubtedly his songs, for these brief compositions show his wit, his inventiveness, his melodic gift, and his unique approach to Americana in the least complex manner. The only problem is one of selection from among the many marvelous songs.

"When General William Booth Enters into Heaven" (text by Vachel Lindsay) is probably the most representative of the lot, for in this song Ives fuses hymn tunes ("washed in the blood of the lamb" is the refrain), clusters of chords in unrelated keys, banjo tunes ("polly wolly doodle"), a bugle call, a folk song, and snatches of well-known tunes. Tonality seems to phase in and out, and the final chord implies no tonal center. The overall mood is jaunty and mock-serious—Booth was a Salvation Army general—and the whole mixture is just delightful.

Other songs equally full of fun are "Circus Band" and "The Side Show," both of which use music-hall style accompaniments replete with all the clichés of the pop piano player of the early 1900s. The words are amusing too—"Cleopatra's on her throne / That golden hair is all her own" is a line from "Circus Band"! In "Side Show" the beat of the singer gets just a bit out of phase with that of the accompaniment, a comic effect harder to achieve deliberately than the listener might imagine.

Many of Ives's more serious songs also use quotes from hymn tunes, pop songs, spirituals, and patriotic songs: "Tom Sails Away," an impressionistic, sad song of parting, has a few bars from George M. Cohan's "Over There"; "They Are There," an original patriotic song, quotes "Columbia, the Gem of the Ocean" and "Tenting Tonight" to a fife obbligato; in "In Flanders Field," a grim war song, we hear "La Marseillaise" as well as "Columbia, the Gem of the Ocean."

"The Children's Hour" and "Two Little Flowers" are simple, innocent, touching little songs devoid of dissonance or complexity; "The Things Our Fathers Loved" and "The Greatest Man" are unabashedly sentimental and nostalgic. In "The Maple Leaves" Ives has the voice half sing, half speak in the manner of Schoenberg's *Pierrot-Lunaire,* but here the effect is of gentle melancholia. At the end of the song the voice falls off in an unaccompanied descending chromatic line with no discernible final tonality. In "The Last Reader" tonality dissolves in the last bars although most of the song is tonal.

One of Ives's most evocative songs is "The Housatonic at Stockbridge," an atmospheric, moody piece of simple serenity. One senses reverie, time suspended, peace.

In each of the songs discussed above, and in his many others, Ives's love for small-town America—her country fairs, Fourth of July celebrations, simple church services, marching bands, circuses, cowboys—rings loud and clear. He was the first major thoroughly American composer.

Dubbed "The Dean of American Composers" by his cohorts and by the public, Aaron Copland (b. 1900) is the most influential of the generation to follow Ives. Although raised in urban New York City (born in Brooklyn) and schooled in Paris under Nadia Boulanger, Copland captured the sounds of the American prairie in abstract works (the middle movement of the Piano Sonata, for example) and in descriptive pieces (*Billy the Kid, Rodeo,* and others). His one major contribution to art song is a group of twelve songs to poems by Emily Dickinson, each of which is dedicated to a fellow composer (1945–50).

The set opens with a quiet paean to "Nature, the gentlest mother"; its "crystalline" (composer's indication) introductory piano figure suggests the wide-open spaces of America's Midwest, and a pastoral mood pervades the song. The widely spaced notes of the last few measures—a favorite Copland device—depict the silence willed by nature at night. The second song begins with scales seven notes apart played simultaneously by the pianist's two hands (the right hand has the tonic A major scale, the left the same scale begun on G sharp not quite one octave below). This cacophonous rush of notes portrays the wind—the song is called "There Came a Wind Like a Bugle"—and sharply clashing sounds continue throughout the song. A fierce, electrifying energy characterizes the music. The third song, "Why Do They Shut Me Out of Heaven? . . . Did I Sing Too Loud?" takes advantage of the whimsical side of Dickinson's poems: the note for the word "loud" is a surprising leap to a G flat from a C flat, and when the line is repeated at the end of the song it goes even higher to an A flat marked f ff (fortississimo!). "The World

Feels Dusty," a quietly philosophical song, is followed by "Heart, we will forget him," a lovely romantic ballad. "Dear March Come In!" is full of exuberant high spirits, while "Sleep Is Supposed to Be" is serene and dignified. Numbers eight ("When they come back"), ten ("I've heard an organ talk sometimes"), and twelve ("The Chariot") are tranquil, but the ninth, "I Felt a Funeral in my Brain," has a heavy, pounding accompaniment that speaks of anxious forboding. The penultimate song, "Going to Heaven!" is an extraordinary outburst of joyous exultation, in which the melodic line rises ecstatically time and time again while the accompaniment rushes up and down the keyboard in canonic triplets. It is a real tour de force for singer and pianist.

The most highly regarded serious composer of art songs among the slightly younger composers is Ned Rorem (b. 1923) who won the Pulitzer Prize in 1976 for *Air Music*, a set of ten variations for orchestra. Rorem is an urban composer —his autobiographical *Paris and New York Diaries of Ned Rorem* make his ties to sophisticated city life all too clear. No wide-open spaces for him, instead the macabre "This Is the House of Bedlam," a mad version of the "House That Jack Built," in which abrupt chords, weird intervals, and surrealistic words compete for attention.

This taste for the macabre, which runs through Rorem's copious output, manifested itself more recently (1971) in the five-song cycle to poems of Sylvia Plath for soprano, clarinet, and piano called *Ariel*. The cycle opens abruptly with loud dissonances for the instruments on the first syllable of the first startling word, "Axes," which is sung to a falling interval of a seventh (D to E flat). The second song begins with an unaccompanied vocal line which hovers on a single note (C), to which it returns for long stretches during the song, and on which it ends, also unaccompanied. Since the subject of the poem is "Poppies in July" and the words refer to the fumes one cannot touch, the opiates, the nauseous capsules, it must be surmised that an opium-induced hypnotic trance is being portrayed musically. Strongest of the five songs is the last, "Lady Lazarus," in which the poet describes her failed suicide attempts. Clearly this is powerful material, suitable for some but by no means all audiences.

Rorem's songs are not all gruesome. "Love's Stricken, 'Why'" (text by Emily Dickinson) from the long cycle *Poems of Love and the Rain* (1962–63) is wistful and tender in its first version (each poem in this "pyramidal" cycle is done twice to contrasting music, and it is impossible to excerpt any one unit from the whole). "Our Youth" is a patter song for trio of singers and piano (words by John Ashbery, 1957) in which non sequiturs are cheerfully sung to comic effect. Nevertheless, songs that make a powerful statement about some phase of modern life are more typical of Rorem, as his grim antiwar cycle *War Scenes* and more personal *Last Poems of Wallace Stevens* (the latter for soprano, cello, and piano) will attest.

It has been said that art songs in English have never achieved the intensity of feeling of the German lieder or the French mélodie. Like most value judgments this is debatable, and—should it seem true at the present time—who knows where or when the next Schubert or the next Chausson will appear? . . .

Interpretation

One of the enduring fascinations of a great piece of music is the way subtle differences in interpretation make of each performance a new experience. Within obvious stylistic limits there is a surprising range of valid interpretative response —expressed by choice of tempo, dynamics, tone color, phrasing, and so forth—for most compositions. Even when a composer tries to give extremely explicit instructions to the performer (Bartok often provides timings exact to a tenth of a second!), no two performances will sound exactly alike.

The reason for this is self-evident—each recreative artist brings his personality, his life experience, his idea of the meaning of the piece, to a performance. An unimaginative performer will give an unimaginative performance even if he or she follows every dynamic indication on the printed page. However, following these instructions will not in itself lead to a robotlike performance, for no two people hear a crescendo, an accent, an accelerando, a pause, in exactly the same way. A pause can be a moment of breathtaking suspense or merely empty space; a crescendo can seem to build with unbearable intensity or simply get louder.

Leaving inadequate artistry aside, even among superior performances vast differences are apparent. Artur Rubinstein's Chopin is warmer, dreamier, more lyrical than Vladimir Horowitz's interpretations, which burn with passionate, almost demonic intensity. Both great pianists play the same notes. They rarely deviate from the composer's specific instructions, and fully appreciate the stylistic demands of nineteenth-century Romantic piano playing. Nevertheless the individual personality of each remains distinct in performance.

How much truer this is of vocal music, where the inexhaustible variety of the timbre and tonal quality of the human voice adds immeasurably to individuality of expression. Even in speech individuals choose different ways to convey a mood, different words to stress, different modes of emphasis, different places to pause. Singers must make infinite numbers of these minute decisions, though many such matters may be determined by instinct rather than reason.

The same artist, if he is indeed an artist and not just a parrot, is unlikely to play or sing the same work twice in exactly the same way. Technical mastery allows a performer to respond freely to spontaneous emotional reactions, as well as to performance conditions.

Often the interaction between singer and accompanist is such that one inspires the other to greater interpretive heights. The superb rendition of Schumann's *Dichterliebe* by Dietrich Fischer-Dieskau with Joerg Demus at the piano, and the remarkable combination of Victoria de los Angeles and Alicia de Larrocha in the Spanish repertoire are but two outstanding examples.

An interesting insight into the differences in interpretation of the same song sung by the same singer with two different pianists is provided by Miss Los Angeles's singing of the tempestuous "Polo" from Falla's *Seven Spanish Popular Songs,* first with that accomplished English accompanist Gerald Moore, and later with a little known Spanish pianist who had been a personal friend of the composer. The latter fairly steams with passion while the former, fine as it is, seems pallid by comparison. Interestingly enough, the performance with Moore was done several years earlier, proving that youth has no monopoly on fiery impetuosity. Often maturity releases smoldering emotions. In any case, unless the artist suffers from arrested development, the years bring subtle changes in interpretation and in vocal color.

For this reason there can be no one definitive performance of any major work. Even when the composer is his or her own interpreter, he or she knows that, if the work is a great one, others will find different and equally valid ways to illumine it.

There have been some great composer-performers and, of course, their recorded performances are treasures. One thinks of Stravinsky conducting *Firebird, Petrouchka, Le Sa-*

cre du Printemps. In the vocal field the closest we come to this phenomenon are two composer-pianists, Benjamin Britten and Francis Poulenc, each of whom had a favorite singer, Peter Pears and Pierre Bernac respectively, for whom he wrote many of his songs and with whom he concertized. These interpretations, many of which are recorded, are also to be treasured.

Occasionally there is a reverse reaction to the obvious identification of a composer with his compositions. Ravel came to despise his all too popular *Boléro* and hated to hear, much less conduct it; Rachmaninov felt the same way about his best known Piano Preludes, although he was usually forced to include at least one as an encore on every recital. In these cases other interpreters would probably provide fresher and more spontaneous performances.

The big debate in our electronic age concerns the relative merits of live and recorded performances. On the one hand the performer, knowing that the slightest error—an intonational lapse, missed note, mispronounced word—which would go unnoticed in a performance will be obvious on a record, and will become very annoying when heard over and over. This might make him tense, too careful, more concerned with accuracy than with expressivity. On the other hand, knowing that an error can be deleted, or that a whole section can be redone as many times as necessary in a recording studio, may free an artist to take chances he wouldn't dare in concert.

In a series of "conversations" with famous singers, Dame Janet Baker revealed that she cannot bear to hear her own records and tapes, and never allowed them to be used in personal appearances. To her the proper performance ambiance is provided only in the concert or opera hall, not the recording studio. Fortunately her adoring record-buying fans feel differently!

In general one is probably more likely to be deeply moved by a great live performance, experienced in the concert hall, than by an equally fine record. The very presence of an artist, his response to the audience, his involvement with the music, and his desire to share his love for it with the audience—these human elements are part of the musical experience.

Of course there is one way to come still closer to the heart of the musical experience, and that is to be one's own interpreter. To sing or play a Schubert or a Schumann cycle, a song by Brahms, Wolf, or Debussy, is to become just a little more human, a little more alive. Since a composition cannot come to life without the intermediary, the performer, each performance is a birth, an act of creation. Man is blessed with few such avenues of gratification.

Glossary of Musical Terms

ADAGIO: Very slow

ALLEGRO: Fast

ANDANTE: slow

ANTIPHONAL: alternate responsive singing or playing; sometimes used for echo effect

ARIOSO: songlike; a combination of declamatory and lyrical singing

ARPEGGIO: the notes of a chord played serially rather than simultaneously

ATONAL: Lacking any tonal center or key

AUGMENTED: enlarged by raising the fifth tone of the triad so that the chord contains two whole steps

BALLAD: a song whose poem is a narrative; a sentimental popular song

BAROQUE: the period in music extending roughly from 1600–1750, whose style is epitomized in the works of Johann Sebastian Bach and Georg Friedrich Händel

BASSO CONTINUO: (also called FIGURED BASS or THOROUGH BASS) an accompaniment improvised from a given bass line; common during the *Baroque* era

CADENCE: a chord progression indicating a close, either full or temporary

CANON: a piece in which one voice imitates the other, the two or more imitative voices entering fairly rapidly one after the other

CANTATA: a vocal composition as opposed to *sonata*; more commonly a religious work employing voices and instruments and including a chorale

CANTILLATION MARKS: notation marks indicating rising and falling melodic fragments, often in preset ornamental figurations; no specific pitch indicated

CANZONET: a short song, often of light character

CHAMBER MUSIC: music for two or more players in groups too small to require a conductor; string quartets, piano trios, wind quintets, and so forth

CHORD: three or more notes played simultaneously

CHROMATICISM: advancing melodically by the smallest intervals possible on the keyboard, that is, half steps; the use of accidentals (notes not in the key signature) to change the harmonies

CODA: literally, a "tail"; an extra section added to a composition after the expected ending

COLORATURA: florid ornamentation in the high vocal ranges

CONSONANCE: a pleasing sound; an accepted chord according to rules of harmony

COUNTERPOINT: (adj.—CONTRAPUNTAL) music consisting of two or more independent horizontal lines; used interchangeably with POLYPHONY (adj.—POLYPHONIC)

COUNTERTENOR: a male voice, produced naturally, with an extremely high range

DA CAPO: an indication to return to the beginning (literally "the head") and repeat the opening section at the conclusion of the piece

DIATONIC: scales composed of patterns of half and whole steps, such as the standard major and minor scales

DISSONANCE: sound unpleasing to the ear; chords not admitted as consonances according to the rules of harmony

DOMINANT: the fifth note of the scale

DOMINANT-SEVENTH: a chord built on the fifth note of the scale with the addition of the seventh note up from the fifth in the key of the original scale; that is, G, B, D, F in the key of C.

EXPOSITION: the first section of a movement in sonata form during which the main themes and tonal centers of the movement are put forth

FERMATA: an indication over a note or rest indicating that the performer should extend the time value according to his own judgment

FIGURED BASS: see *basso continuo*

FIORITURA: the Italian word for highly ornamented singing

FUGUE: a short composition in which one theme is introduced by the first "voice" (the term is used even when referring to instruments) and then imitated contrapuntally by the other voices; the texture thus consists of interwoven independent melodic strands

HARMONY: the combining of notes into chords; the combination of chords into progressions

HOMOPHONY: the stressing of one main melodic line, usually in the top voice, and the supporting of that melodic line by appropriate chords

INTERVAL: the distance in pitch between any two notes

INVERSION: positions other than root position (the tonic note on the bottom) of chords; turning upside down of intervals previously used

LARGO: very slow—the slowest tempo indication

LAY (LAI): a song, a ballad

LEGATO: connected

LENTO: very slow but not as slow as *largo*

MADRIGAL: originally a short pastoral poem or a song based on such a poem; by the fourteenth century, a secular piece for two or more independent voices

MAJOR: the scale based on the pattern tonic, two whole steps and one-half, three whole steps and a final half

MELISMATIC: decoratively melodic

MINOR: 1. **natural**—formed by lowering the third, sixth, and seventh notes of the major scale; gives key signature

2. **harmonic**—formed by lowering only the third and sixth notes of the major scale

3. **melodic**—formed by lowering only the third note of the major scale on the way up and the third, sixth, and seventh notes on the way down

MODAL: based on scale patterns or modes other than major or minor

MODULATION: moving from one tonal center to another

MONODIST: a composer who favors a simple *homophonic* style of writing

MOTET: an elaborate composition, very popular in the Middle Ages, in which a tune is much embroidered by polyphonic and often polytextual interweaving

OBBLIGATO: an accompanying instrumental passage essential to the music

OPUS: literally "work"; opus numbers are assigned to works by composers to indicate chronology of composition or publication

ORATORIO: a large composition involving soloists, chorus, and orchestra to a text derived from the Bible

OSTINATO: literally "stubborn"; a figure repeated persistently

PEDAL POINT: the sustaining or repetition of one note for a long period of time

POLYPHONY: see *counterpoint*

POSTLUDE: a section occurring after the main body of the work is finished; particularly a concluding section of a song for the piano after the vocal line has ended

PRELUDE: an introductory section; a short composition used to introduce a suite or another composition; sometimes used as title of short independent piece

PRESTO: very fast

RECAPITULATION: repeat; final section of movement in sonata form in which main themes are repeated

RECITATIVE: declamatory as opposed to lyric

RITARD: slowing down of tempo

RONDEAU: a short song based on a poem whose opening and closing are identical

SCHERZO: literally "joke"; a movement or independent composition of a jocular nature

SEQUENCE: the repetition of a given pattern on different pitch levels

SONATA: a composition to be played rather than sung; a composition in two or more movements for one or two instruments

SONATA FORM: a structure consisting of three main sections, exposition, development, and recapitulation

SOSTENUTO: sustained

STACCATO: short, disconnected

STROPHIC: adjective describing a song in which the same music is used for each verse of the poem

SUSPENSION: a discord produced by retaining one or more notes of a chord while the other notes progress to the next chord

SYNCOPATION: an accent on a weak beat; a displaced accent

TARANTELLA: an Italian dance in 6/8 time

TONIC: the first note of a scale

TREMOLO: an effect produced by rapidly alternating octaves on the piano, by rapid repetition of a single note on a string instrument

TRIAD: the COMMON CHORD; the first, third, and fifth notes of a scale played simultaneously

TWELVE TONAL: granting equal importance to each of the twelve tones so that no one tonal center or key is suggested

VIOLA DA GAMBA: precursor of the cello, played held between the knees

VIVACE: lively

WHOLE-TONE SCALE: scale pattern based on all whole steps

Index of Composers and Works

A

Abendempfindung (Evening Song), Mozart, 41, 46–7

Abschiedslied der Zugvögel (Farewell Song of the Birds of Passage), Mendelssohn, 84

Adelaide, Beethoven, 49, 51

Adieu (Farewell), Fauré, 129–30

Adieux de la hôtesse (The Hostess's Farewells), Bizet, 125

Again, as Before, Alone, Tchaikovsky, 167

Ah! nelle sorti umane (Ah! In Human Destinies), Händel, 31–2

Albéniz, Isaac, 173, 175

Alone with the Sea, Bartók, 180

Als Luise die Briefe ihres ungetreuen Liebhabers verbrannte (When Louise Burned the Letters of Her Unfaithful Lover), Mozart, 41, 47–8

Alt deutsches Frülingslied (Old German Spring Song), Mendelssohn, 83

Amor y Odio (Love and Hate), Granados, 174

Amour d'antan (Love of Yesteryear), Chausson, 134

An Chloë (To Chloe), Mozart, 41, 44

An die ferne Geliebte (To the Distant Beloved), Beethoven, 50, 53–4, 188

An die Hoffnung (To Hope), Beethoven, 49, 52–3

An die Musik (To Music), Schubert, 59

An Leukon (To Leukon), Berg, 118

An meinem Herzen, an meiner Brust (On My Heart, On My Breast), Schumann, 77

Anthology of Italian Songs, 26

Antiphon, Vaughn Williams, 185

Apaisement (Appeasement), Chausson, 135

Apparition, Debussy, 142–3

Après un rêve (After a Dream), Fauré, 128

Ariadne auf Naxos, Strauss, 104, 109

Ariel, Rorem, 192

Ash Grove, Britten, 187

Asturiana, Falla, 175

At the Bier of a Young Woman, Grieg, 177

At the Brook, Dvořák, 178

At the Round Earth's Imagined Corners, Britten, 188

Au bord de l'eau (At the Edge of the Water), Fauré, 129

Auf dem Wasser zu singen (To Be Sung on the Waters), Schubert, 59, 62–3

Auf Flügeln des Gesanges (On Wings of Song), Mendelssohn, 81

Auric, Georges, 155

Aus! Aus! (Away! Away!), Mahler, 105–6

Automne (Autumn), Fauré, 129
Avant le cinéma (Before the
    Cinema), Poulenc, 158
Ariettes oubliées (Forgotten
    Songs), Debussy, 142, 144

B

B Minor Mass, Bach, 29
Babi Yar, Shostakovich, 170–1
Bach, Johann Sebastian, 28–30,
    36, 58, 120
  B Minor Mass, 29
Balakirev, Mily Alexeyevich, 165
Ballade des gros dindons (Ballad
    of the Fat Turkeys),
    Chabrier, 151
Ballade que fait Villon à la
    requeste de sa mere pour
    prier Nostre-Dame (Ballad
    Made by Villon at the
    Request of his Mother to
    Pray to The Virgin Mary),
    Debussy, 141, 147–8
Banalités (Banalities), Poulenc,
    158
Bartok, Béla, 90, 177, 179, 180,
    194
  Alone with the Sea, 180
  My Bed is Calling, 180
  The Sound of Autumn, 180
Batter my Heart, Britten, 187
Beethoven, Ludwig van, 16, 34,
    48–55, 58, 102, 188
  Adelaide, 49, 51
  An die ferne Geliebte, 50, 53–4,
    188
  An die Hoffnung, 49, 52–3
  Choral Fantasy, 49
  Der Floh, 49, 50, 52
  Der Kuss, 50, 54–5
  Die Ehre Gottes aus der Natur,
    49–51

Fidelio, 49
  Missa Solemnis, 49
Begegnung (The Meeting), Wolf,
    95–6
Berceuse (Lullaby), Bizet, 126
Berg, Alban, 58, 110–120
  An Leukon, 118
  Five Songs for Voice and
    Orchestra, 118
  Four Songs, 118, 120
  Lulu, 118
  Schliesse mir die Augen beide,
    118–120
  Seven Early Songs, 118
  Wozzeck, 118
Berlioz, Hector, 102–3, 121–123
  La Captive, 123
  Nuits d'été, 122
  Quand tu chantes, 123
  Sur les lagunes, 122
  Zaïde, 123
Biblical Songs, Dvořák, 178
Billy Budd, Britten, 186
Binchois, Gilles, 21
Bizet, Georges, 121, 124–6, 128,
    173
  Adieux de la hôtesse, 125
  Berceuse, 126
  Carmen, 125–7
  J'aime l'amour, 126
  Vous ne priez pas, 124–5
Black Roses, Sibelius, 181
The Blessed Virgin's
    Expostulation, Purcell, 27
Boris Godunov, Moussorgsky,
    163
Borodin, Alexander, 160, 162–2,
    165, 167
  Pride, 162
  Sea Princess, 162
  Sleeping Beauty, 162
Brahms, Johannes, 14, 58, 84–92,

98, 102, 111, 121
Die Mainacht, 86–8
Geheimnis, 86, 89
Geistliches Wiegenlied, 91
In stiller Nacht, 86, 91
Liebeslieder Waltzes, 14, 85,
   91–2
Mädchenlied, 86, 89–90
Mein Mädel hat einen
   Rosenmund, 86, 90
O wüsst' ich doch den Weg
   zurück, 86, 88–9
Requiem, 87
Treue Liebe, 86–7
Vier ernste Gesänge, 85–6
Bredon Hall, Vaughn Williams,
   186
Britten, Benjamin, 14, 186–8, 196
   Ash Grove, 187
   At the Round Earth's Imagined
     Corners, 188
   Batter My Heart, 187
   Billy Budd, 186
   Death Be Not Proud, 188
   Death in Venice, 186
   The Holy Sonnets of John
     Donne, 187
   Oh Might These Sighs and
     Tears, 187
   Oh My Black Soul, 187
   Oh, to Vex Me, 187
   Oliver Cromwell is Buried and
     Dead, 187
   Peter Grimes, 186
   Prodigal Son, 186
   Sally Gardens, 187
   Seven Sonnets of Michelangelo,
     187
   Songs and Proverbs of William
     Blake, 187
   Thou Hast Made Me, 187
Bruckner, Anton, 102

Byrd, William, 21

C

Caldara, Antonio, 23
The Call, Vaughn Williams, 185
Cancion (Song), Falla, 175
Canciones amatorias (Love
   Songs), Granados, 173
Canciones sobre textos castillanos
   (Songs on Castillian Texts),
   Rodrigo, 176
Cantique à l'épouse (Canticle to
   the Wife), Chausson, 133
Canto a Sevilla (Song to Seville),
   Turina, 176
Carmen, Bizet, 125–7
Carmina Burana, Orff, 19
Catalogue des fleurs (Flower
   Catalogue), Milhaud, 156
Cesti, Marc'Antonio, 23, 26
C'est le joli printemps (Here is the
   Pretty Spring), Poulenc, 157
C'est l'extase (This is Ecstasy),
   Debussy, 141–2, 144–5
Chabrier, Emmanuel, 151, 173
   Ballade des gros dindons, 151
   Pastorale des petits cochons
     roses, 151
   Villanelle des petits canards,
     151
Chaminade, Cécile, 153–4
Chanson à boire (Drinking
   Song), Ravel, 153
Chanson de la fille frivole (Song
   of the Frivolous Girl),
   Poulenc, 157
Chanson du pêcheur (Fisherman's
   Song), Fauré, 122, 128
Chanson épique (Epic Song),
   Ravel, 153
Chanson romanesque

(continued)
   (Romanesque Song), Ravel,
      153
Chansons de Bilitis (Songs of
   Bilitis), Debussy, 149
Chansons de France (Songs of
   France), Debussy, 149
Chansons gaillardes (Risqué
   Songs), Poulenc, 158
Chansons madécasses
   (Madagascan Songs), Ravel,
   14, 152–3
Chansons villageoises (Village
   Songs), Poulenc, 157–8
Chant de nourrice (The
   Nursemaid's Song),
   Milhaud, 157
Chants populaires hébraïques
   (Popular Hebrew Songs),
   Milhaud, 156
The Chariot, Copland, 192
Chausson, Ernest, 97, 121, 124,
   127, 128, 133–137, 154, 159
   Amour d'antan, 134
   Apaisement, 135
   Cantique à l'épouse, 133
   Dans la forêt du charme et de
      l'enchantement, 133
   La Caravane, 135–6
   Le Colibri, 134
   Le Printemps, 134–5
   Les Heures, 136
   Nanny, 134
   Nocturne, 134
   Nos souvenirs, 134
   Serre d'ennui, 136
   Serres chaudes, 136
The Children's Hour, Ives, 190
Choice Ayres, Purcell, 26
Choral Fantasy, Beethoven, 49
Christ is Risen, Rachmaninov,
   168

Cinq Mélodies grèque populaires
   (Five Popular Greek
   Melodies), Ravel, 151
Circus Band, Ives, 190
Clair de lune (Moonlight),
   Debussy, 130, 142, 145
Clair de lune (Moonlight), Fauré,
   130, 145
The Classicist, Moussorgsky, 164
Colloque sentimental
   (Sentimental Colloquy),
   Debussy, 142, 146–7
Come Away Death, Sibelius, 181
Comme Dieu rayonne (How
   Radiant is God), Fauré, 132
Copland, Aaron, 191–2
   The Chariot, 192
   Dear March Come In! 192
   Going to Heaven, 192
   Heart, We Will Forget Him,
      192
   I Felt a Funeral in my Brain,
      192
   I've Heard an Organ Talk
      Sometimes, 192
   Nature, The Gentlest Mother,
      191
   Sleep is Supposed to Be, 192
   There Came a Wind Like a
      Bugle, 191
   When They Come Back, 192
   Why Do They Shut Me Out of
      Heaven? 191
   The World Feels Dusty, 192
Creation, Haydn, 34
Crépuscule (Twilight), Fauré, 132
Couperin, Francois, 120
Cui, César Antonovitch, 165

D

Dank (Thanks), Schoenberg, 111
Dans la forêt du charme et de

l'enchantement (In the Forest of Charm and Enchantment), Chausson, 133

Dans un parfum de roses blanches (In a Perfume of White Roses), Fauré, 132

Dargomizhsky, Alexander, 160–1
  I am Grieving, 161
  The Stone Guest, 161

Darling Savishna, Moussorgsky, 164

Das Buch der hängenden Gärten (The Book of the Hanging Gardens), Schoenberg, 110, 113–5

Das Leben ist ein Traum (Life is a Dream), Haydn, 36–7

Das Lied von der Erde (Songs of the Earth), Mahler, 104

Das Veilchen (The Violet), Mozart, 41, 44–6

Das verlassene Mägdlein (The Foresaken Maiden), Wolf, 95–7

Das Zitternde Glänzen der spielenden Wellen (The Shimmering Sparkle of Frolicsome Waves), Händel, 33–4

Dear March Come In! Copland, 192

Death Be Not Proud, Britten, 188

Death in Venice, Britten, 186

Death of the Poet, Shostakovich, 172

Debussy, Claude, 97, 100, 112, 114, 121, 127–8, 130, 141–149, 154, 159, 162, 173, 175, 183
  Apparition, 142–3
  Ariettes oubliées, 142–144
  Ballade que fait Villon à la

requeste de sa mère pour prier Nostre-Dame, 141, 147–8
  C'est l'extase, 141–2, 144–5
  Chansons de Bilitis, 149
  Chansons de France, 149
  Claire de lune, 130, 142, 145
  Colloque sentimental, 142, 146–7
  De rêve, 142, 145–6
  En sourdine, 130
  Fantoches, 141
  Fêtes galantes, 142
  Green, 130
  Harmonie du soir, 142–4
  Il pleure dans mon coeur, 130
  La Chevelure, 141
  Le Jet d'eau, 141
  Mandoline, 141–2
  Noël des enfants qui n'ont plus de maisons, 141
  Pantomime, 141
  Pelléas et Mélisande, 141, 144
  Proses lyriques, 142
  Trois Ballades de François Villon, 142
  Voici que le printemps, 141

Dedication, Turina, 175

Delius, Frederick, 182–3
  The Homeward Way, 182
  Il pleure dans mon coeur, 183
  La Lune blanche, 183
  Le Ciel est par-dessus le toit, 183
  Sea Drift, 183
  Songs from the Norwegian, 182
  Three Verlaine Songs, 183

De Profundis, Shostakovich, 171

Der Corregidor (The Corridor), Wolf, 94

Der Doppelgänger (The Shadow of Death), Schubert, 59, 69

Der Erlkönig (The Erlking),
Loewe, 57
Der Erlkönig, Reichardt, 55
Der Erlkönig, Schubert, 59, 61–2,
67
Der Erlkönig, Zelter, 55
De rêve (Dream), Debussy, 142,
145–6
Der Floh (The Flea), Beethoven,
49, 50, 52
Der Freischütz, Weber, 56
Der greise Kopf (The Gray
Head), Schubert, 65
Der Hirt auf dem Felsen (The
Shepherd on the Rock),
Schubert, 14, 55, 59, 70–1
Der Kuss (The Kiss), Beethoven,
50, 54–5
Der Leiermann (The Organ
Grinder), Schubert, 59, 67–8
Der Lindenbaum (The Linden
Tree), Schubert, 59, 65, 79–
80
Der Nussbaum (The Walnut
Tree), Schumann, 73, 79–80,
89
Der Rosenkavalier, Strauss, 104,
109
Der Tod und das Mädchen
(Death and the Maiden),
Schubert, 59
Der Wanderer, Schubert, 59
Der Wegweiser (The Signpost),
Schubert, 67
Der Zauberer (The Magician),
Mozart, 41, 43–44
Des Antonius von Padua
Fischpredigt (St. Antony of
Padua's Sermon to the Fish),
Mahler, 104
Des Knaben Wunderhorn (The
Youth's Magic Horn),
Mahler, 103–4
Des Pres, Josquin, 21
Deux Mélodies hébraïques (Two
Hebrew Melodies), Ravel,
151
Dialogues des Carmélites,
Poulenc, 157
The Diary of One Who Vanished,
Janáček, 179
Dichterliebe (The Poet's Love),
Schumann, 72, 73, 195
Dido and Aneas, Purcell, 26–7
Die Alte (The Old Woman),
Mozart, 44
Die beiden Grenadiere (The Two
Grenadiers), Schumann, 73,
78
Die Ehre Gottes aus der Natur
(Praise of God from Nature,
or Creation's Hymn),
Beethoven, 49–51
Die Forelle (The Trout),
Schubert, 59, 62
Die ihr schwebet um diese Palmen
(Among the Floating Palms),
Wolf, 95, 98
Die kleine Spinnerin (The Little
Spinner), Mozart, 41–3
Die Krähe (The Raven),
Schubert, 67
Die Liebe liebt das Wandern
(Love Likes to Wander),
Schubert, 65
Die Mainacht (May Night),
Brahms, 86–8
Die Post (The Postman),
Schubert, 59, 66–7
Die schöne Mullerin (The Sweet
Maid of the Mill), Schubert,
59, 63–4
D'Indy, Vincent, 175
Does the Day Dawn,

Tchaikovsky, 166
Don Quichotte à Dulcinée (Don Quixote to Dulcinee), Ravel, 153
Dos canciones (Two Songs), Turina, 175
Doubt, Glinka, 161
Dowland, John, 22
The Dream of Gerontius, Elgar, 183–4
Dufay, Guillaume, 21
Dunstable, John, 21
Duparc, Henri, 97, 121, 124, 127, 128, 133, 137–140, 154, 159
  Extase, 137
  Lamento, 137, 139
  La Vague et la cloche, 137, 139–40
  L'Invitation au voyage, 137–8
  Phydilé, 137
  Soupir, 137–9
  Testament, 137
Durey, Louis, 155
Du Ring an meinem Finger (You Ring on my Finger), Schumann, 73, 75
Dvořák, Antonín, 177–8
  At the Brook, 178
  Biblical Songs, 178
  The Forsaken Lassie, 178
  Gypsy Songs, 178
  Leave Me Alone, 178
  The Maiden's Lament, 178
  Moravian Duets, 178
  Songs My Mother Taught Me, 178

E

Einsamkeit (Solitude), Schubert, 65
El Amor Brujo (The Sorcerer's Love), Falla, 175

Elektra, Strauss, 104
Elfenlied (The Elves' Song), Wolf, 95, 97–98
Elgar, Sir Edward, 182–4
  The Dream of Gerontius, 183–4
Elijah, Mendelssohn, 80
El Majo Discreto (The Discreet Majo), Granados, 174
El Majo Timido (The Timid Majo), Granados, 174
El Mirar de la Maja (The Maja's Mirror), Granados, 174
El Tra la la y el Punteado, Granados, 174
En sourdine (Muted), Debussy, 130
En sourdine (Muted), Fauré, 130
Er, der Herrlichste von allen (The Most Glorious of All), Schumann, 74
Erstarrung (Benumbed), Schubert, 65
Erwartung (Expectation), Schoenberg, 112, 115
Esther, Händel, 29
Extase (Ecstasy), Duparc, 137

F

Falla, Manuel de, 173–5, 195
  Asturiana, 175
  Cancion, 175
  El Amor Brujo, 175
  Jota, 175
  Nana, 175
  Polo, 195
  Seguidilla murciana, 175
  Seven Spanish Popular Songs, 175, 195
  Trois Mélodies, 174
The False Note, Borodin, 162

Fantoches (Puppets), Debussy, 141

The Fatal Hour Comes on Apace, Purcell, 27

Fauré, Gabriel, 97, 100, 121, 122, 126–133, 134–5, 137, 145, 154, 159, 183
　Adieu, 129–30
　Après un rêve, 128
　Au bord de l'eau, 129
　Automne, 129
　Chanson du pêcheur, 122, 128
　Clair de lune, 130, 145
　Comme Dieu rayonne, 132
　Crépuscule, 132
　Dans un parfum de roses blanches, 132
　En sourdine, 130
　Green, 130
　J'ai presque peur, 131
　J'allais par des chemins perfides, 131
　La Bonne Chanson, 130–2, 135
　L'Absent, 129
　La Chanson d'Eve, 132
　La Lune blanche luit dans les bois, 131, 135
　Le Jardin clos, 132
　Lydia, 129
　Mandoline, 130
　Nell, 129
　O Mort, poussière d'étoiles, 132
　Paradis, 132
　Poème d'un jour, 129
　Prison, 130
　Rencontre, 129
　Roses ardentes, 132
　Sérénade toscane, 128
　Spleen, 130
　Toujours, 129–30
Faust, Gounod, 123, 126

Fêtes galantes, Debussy, 142
Fidelio, Beethoven, 49
The First Kiss, Sibelius, 181
The Five, 165
Five Mystical Songs, Vaughn Williams, 185
Five Songs for Voice and Orchestra, Berg, 118
Five Songs Without Words, Prokofiev, 169
The Flea, Moussorgsky, 164
Florentine School, 22
The Forest, Kodály, 180
The Forsaken Lassie, Dvořák, 178
Four Songs, Berg, 118, 120
Four Songs With Orchestra, Schoenberg, 117
Franck, César, 121, 124, 155
Frauenliebe und Leben (The Love and Life of a Woman), Schumann, 72, 73, 74–8
Frühlingslied (Song of Spring), Mendelssohn, 83

G

Ganymed, Schubert, 59
Gefor'ne Thränen (Frozen Tears), Schubert, 65
Geheimnis (Mystery), Brahms, 86, 89
Geh' Geliebter, geh' jetzt (Go, Beloved, Go Now), Wolf, 95, 99
Geistliches Wiegenlied (Spiritual Lullaby), Brahms, 91
The General, Moussorgksy, 164
German Songs, Händel, 29, 30
German Songs, Spohr, 55
Giu nei tartarei regni (Down in the Tartarean Realm), Händel, 30–1
Glazunov, Alexander, 167

Oriental Romance, 167
Glinka, Mikhail, 160, 161, 173
  Doubt, 161
  The Lark, 161
  A Life for the Tsar, 161
  Russlan and Ludmila, 161
Gloria, Poulenc, 157
Going to Heaven, Copland, 192
Good Friday, Holst, 186
Gounod, Charles, 121, 123–6
  Faust, 123, 126
  Medjé or La Chanson arabe,
    123–4
  Venise, 123
Granados, Enrique, 173–4
  Amor y Odio, 174
  Canciones amatorias, 173
  El Majo Discreto, 174
  El Majo Timido, 174
  El Mirar de la Maja, 174
  El Tra la la y el Punteado, 174
  La Maja de Goya, 174
  La Maja dolorosa, 174
  Tonadillas al Estilo Antiguo,
    173–4
The Greatest Man, Ives, 190
Green, Debussy, 130
Green, Fauré, 130
Greensleeves, Vaughn Williams,
  184
Grieg, Edvard, 176–7, 182
  At the Bier of a Young Woman,
    177
  Hidden Love, 176
  I Love You, 176
  The Princess, 177
  Radiant Night, 177
  Ragnheld, 177
  Springtime, 177
  With a Water Lily, 177
  Woodland Wandering, 177
Griffes, Charles, 189

Gypsy Songs, Dvořák, 178
Gretchen am Spinnrade
    (Gretchen at the Spinning
    Wheel), Schubert, 43, 59–61

H

Had I Only Known,
    Tchaikovsky, 166
Hahn, Reynaldo, 154
Händel, Georg Friedrich, 25,
    28–34, 35, 120, 159, 184
  Ah! nelle sorti umane, 31–2
  Das Zitternde Glänzen der
    spielenden Wellen, 33–4
  Esther, 29
  German Songs, 29, 30
  Giu nei tartarei regni, 30–1
  Israel in Egypt, 29
  Italian Duets, 30
  Judas Maccabaeus, 29
  Messiah, 29–30
  Samson, 29
  Se tu non lasci amore, 32–3
Harmonie du soir (Harmony of
    the Evening), Debussy,
    142–4
The Harvest of Sorrow,
    Rachmaninov, 168
Haydn, Franz Joseph, 34–40, 41,
    50, 102, 159
  Creation, 34
  Das Leben ist ein Traum, 36–7
  My Mother Bids me Bind my
    Hair, 36, 38–9
  She Never Told her Love, 36–7
  The Spirit's Song, 36, 39–40
Heart, We Will Forget Him,
    Copland, 192
Heidenröslein (Little Meadow
    Rose), Schubert, 59
Heimliche Aufforderung (The

(continued)
    Secret Invitation), Strauss,
    105, 109
Helft mir, ihr Schwestern (Help
    Me, My Sisters), Schumann,
    75–6
Herbstlied (Autumn Song),
    Mendelssohn, 83–4
Hexenlied (Witches' Song),
    Mendelssohn, 81–2
Hidden Love, Grieg, 176
Hiller, Johann, 55
Hirtenlied (Shepherd's Song),
    Mendelssohn, 83
Histoires naturelles (Nature
    Stories), Ravel, 150
Holst, Gustav, 184,186
    Good Friday, 186
    Intercession, 186
    I Sing of a Maiden, 186
    Six Medieval Lyrics, 186
The Holy Sonnets of John Donne,
    Britten, 187
The Homeward Way, Delius, 182
Honegger, Arthur, 155
Hotel, Poulenc, 158
The Housatonic at Stockbridge,
    Ives, 190
Hüe, Georges, 154
Hymne, Poulenc, 158

I

I am Grieving, Dargomizhsky,
    161
Ich ging mit Lust durch einen
    grünen Wald (I Went with
    Joy through a Green Wood),
    Mahler, 104–5
Ich kann's nicht fassen, nicht
    glauben (I Cannot Grasp or
    Believe It), Schumann, 75
I Felt a Funeral in my Brain,

Copland, 192
If Music Be the Food of Love,
    Purcell, 27
I Got Me Flowers, Vaughn
    Williams, 185
I Love and I Must, Purcell, 27–8
I Love You, Grieg, 176
Il pleure dans mon coeur (My
    Heart Cries), Debussy, 130
Il pleure dans mon coeur, Delius,
    183
In Flanders Field, Ives, 190
In stiller Nacht (In Stillest
    Night), Brahms, 86, 91
Intercession, Holst, 186
In the Silence of the Night,
    Rachmaninov, 168
Isaac, Heinrich, 21
I Sing of a Maiden, Holst, 186
Is my Team Ploughing? Vaughn
    Williams, 186
Israel in Egypt, Händel, 29
Italian Duets, Händel, 30
Italienisches Liederbuch (Italian
    Songbook), Wolf, 93, 95, 100
I've Heard an Organ Talk
    Sometimes, Copland, 192
Ives, Charles, 189–91
    The Children's Hour, 190
    Circus Band, 190
    The Greatest Man, 190
    The Housatonic at Stockbridge,
        190
    In Flanders Field, 190
    The Last Reader, 190
    The Maple Leaves, 190
    The Side Show, 190
    They are There, 190
    The Things our Fathers Loved,
        190
    Tom Sails Away, 190
    Two Little Flowers, 190

When General William Booth
Enters Into Heaven, 189

J

J'aime l'amour (I Love Love),
Bizet, 126
J'ai presque peur (I'm Almost
Afraid), Fauré, 131
J'allais par des chemins perfides
(I Went in Perfidious Ways),
Fauré, 131
Janáček, Leŏs, 177–9
The Diary of One Who
Vanished, 179
Jenufa, 178
Slavonic Mass, 178
Jenufa, Janáček, 178
Jesus Bettelt (Jesus Begs),
Schoenberg, 112
Jota, Falla, 175
Judas Maccabaeus, Händel, 29

K

Kindertotenlieder (Songs on the
Death of Children), Mahler,
104, 106
Kodály, Zoltan, 90, 177, 179–80
The Forest, 180
Sappho's Love Song, 180
Kol Nidrei, Schoenberg, 118

L

La Bonne Chanson (The Good
Song), Fauré, 130–2, 135
L'Absent (The Absent One),
Fauré, 129
La Captive, Berlioz, 123
La Caravane, Chausson, 135–6
La Chanson d'Eve (Eve's Song),
Fauré, 132
La Chevelure (The Hair),

Debussy, 141
Lady Lazarus, Rorem, 193
Lalo, Eduoard, 173
La Lune blanche (The White
Moon), Delius, 183
La Lune blanche luit dans les bois
(The White Moon Shines in
the Woods), Fauré, 131, 135
La Maja de Goya, Granados, 174
La Maja dolorosa (The Sad
Maja), Granados, 174
Lamento, Duparc, 137, 139
The Lark, Glinka, 161
Las Locas por amor (Crazy for
Love), Turina, 175
Last Poems of Wallace Stevens,
Rorem, 193
The Last Reader, Ives, 190
La Vague et la cloche (The Wave
and the Bell), Duparc, 137,
139–40
Leave Me Alone, Dvořák, 178
Le Bestiaire (The Fable Book),
Poulenc, 151
Le Ciel est par-dessus le toit (The
Sky Is Above the Roof),
Delius, 183
Le Colibri (The Hummingbird),
Chausson, 134
Le Gars qui vont à la fête (The Kid
Who Goes to the Fair),
Poulenc, 157
Le Jardin clos (The Hidden
Garden), Fauré, 132
Le Jet d'eau (The Fountain),
Debussy, 141
Le Mendiant (The Begger),
Poulenc, 157
Le Printemps (Springtime),
Chausson, 134–5
Les Heures (The Hours),
Chausson, 136

Les Six, 153, 155, 158, 169
Le Souris (The Mouse), Poulenc,
    158
Let Beauty Awake, Vaughn
    Williams, 185
Liebeslieder Waltzes (Lovesong
    Waltzes), Brahms, 14, 85,
    91–2
Lieder eines fahrenden Gesellen
    (Songs of the Wayfarer),
    Mahler, 14, 103–4, 106
Liederkreis (Song Cycle),
    Schumann, 72–3
Lieder und Gesänge aus der
    Jugendzeit (Songs and Airs
    of Youth), Mahler, 103–4
Liede vom Winde (Song of the
    Wind), Wolf, 97
A Life for the Tsar, Glinka, 161
Lilacs, Rachmaninov, 168
Linden Lea, Vaughn Williams,
    184
L'Invitation au voyage (Invitation
    to a Journey), Duparc, 137–8
Liszt, Franz, 102–3
Loewe, Karl, 55, 57, 97
    Der Erlkönig, 57
Lorelei, Shostakovich, 171
Lotti, Antonio, 23
Love's Stricken "Why", Rorem,
    193
Lullaby, Moussorgsky, 163
Lully, Jean Baptiste, 22
Lullu, Berg, 118
Lydia, Fauré, 129

M

MacDowell, Edward, 188–9
Machaut, Guillaume de, 20
Machines agricoles (Agricultural
    Machinery), Milhaud, 156
Madam, Look, Shostakovich, 171
Mädchenlied (A Maiden's Song),
    Brahms, 86, 89–90
Madrigales amatorios (Madrigals
    of Love), Rodrigo, 176
Mahler, Gustav, 14, 58, 92,
    102–109, 111, 169
    Aus! Aus!, 105–6
    Das Lied von der Erde, 104
    Des Antonius von Padua
        Fischpredigt, 104
    Des Knaben Wunderhorn,
        103–4
    Ich ging mit Lust durch einen
        grünen Wald, 104–5
    Kindertotenlieder, 104, 106
    Lieder eines fahrenden
        Gesellen, 14, 103–4, 106
    Lieder und Gesänge aus der
        Jugendzeit, 103–4
The Maiden's Lament, Dvořák,
    178
Maiglöckchen und die Blümenlein
    (The Maybell and the
    Flowers), Mendelssohn, 84
Malaguena, Shostakovich, 171
Mandoline, Debussy, 141–2
Mandoline, Fauré, 130
Manuel Venegas, Wolf, 94
The Maple Leaves, Ives, 190
Medjé ou La Chanson arabe
    (Medjé or The Arab Song),
    Gounod, 123–4
Mein Herz ist stumm (My Heart
    is Silent), Strauss, 105,
    108–109
Mein Liebster singt (My Love
    Sings), Wolf, 95, 101
Mein Mädel hat einen
    Rosenmund (My Maiden
    Has a Rosebud Mouth),
    Brahms, 86, 90
Mendelssohn, Felix, 80–84, 102,
    135
    Abschiedslied der Zugvögel, 84

Alt deutches Frülingslied, 83
Auf Flugeln des Gesanges, 81
Elijah, 80
Frülingslied, 83
Herbstlied, 83–4
Hexenlied, 81–2
Hirtenlied, 83
Maiglöckchen und die
    Blümenlein, 84
Neue Liebe, 81–2
Reiselied, 82–3
Schilflied, 83
Volkslied, 84
Wedding March, 135
Zweistimmige Lieder, 84
Messiah, Händel, 29–30
Milhaud, Darius, 149, 155–7
    Catalogue des fleurs, 156
    Chant de nourrice, 157
    Chants populaires
    hébraïques, 156
    Machines agricoles, 156
    Poèmes juifs, 156
Missa Solemnis, Beethoven, 49
Mondnacht (Moonlit Night),
    Schumann, 73, 79
Monteverdi, Claudio, 22
Moravian Duets, Dvořák, 178
Moses und Aron, Schoenberg,
    118
Moussorgsky, Modest, 49, 160,
    161–5, 167, 171
    Boris Godunov, 163
    The Classicist, 164
    Darling Savishna, 164
    The Flea, 164
    The General, 164
    Lullaby, 163
    Pride, 165
    The Seminarist, 164
    Serenade, 163
    Shall A Man Spin? 165
    Softly the Spirit Flew Up to

Heaven, 165
    Songs and Dances of Death,
    163
    Trepak, 163
    You Drunken Sot, 164
Mozart, Wolfgang Amadeus, 25,
    34, 40–8, 50, 55, 58, 102, 159
    Abendempfindung, 41, 46–7
    Als Luise die Briefe ihres
    ungetreuen Liebhabers
    verbrannte, 41, 47–8
    An Chloë, 41, 44
    Das Veilchen, 41, 44–6
    Der Zauberer, 41, 43–4
    Die Alte, 44
    Die kleine Spinnerin, 41–3
    Sehnsucht nach dem Frühling,
    41–2
    Trennungslied, 44
My Mother Bids me Bind My
    Hair, Haydn, 36, 38–9
My Bed is Calling, Bartok, 180
Myrthen (Myrtle), Schumann,
    72–3

N

Nana, Falla, 175
Nanny, Chausson, 134
Nature, the Gentlest Mother,
    Copland, 191
Nell, Fauré, 129
Neue Liebe (New Love),
    Mendelssohn, 81–2
Nielsen, Carl, 178, 181–2
Night, Rubinstein, 167
Nixe Binsefuss (Mermaid of the
    Marshes), Wolf, 97
Nocturne, Chausson, 134
Nöel des enfants qui n'ont plus de
    maisons (Christmas of
    Children Who No Longer
    Have Homes), Debussy, 141
Nos souvenirs (Our Memories),

Chausson, 134

Not All My Torments, Purcell,
27–8

Nuits d'été (Summer Nights),
Berlioz, 122

Nun hast du mir den ersten
Schmerz getan (Thus You
Have Caused Me the First
Pain), Schumann, 76–8

Nun ist die Welt so trübe (But
Now the World is Dreary),
Schubert, 65

O

Oberon, Weber, 56

O Cessate di Piagarmi (Oh No
Longer Seek to Pain Me),
Scarlatti, 25

O Delvig, Delvig, Shostakovich,
172

Ode to Napoleon, Schoenberg,
118

Oh, Do Not Grieve,
Rachmaninov, 168

Oh Might These Sighs and Tears,
Britten, 187

Oh My Blacke Soule, Britten, 187

Oh, Never Sing to Me Again,
Rachmaninov, 167

Oh, To Vex Me, Britten, 187

Oh, When I Was in Love with
You, Vaughn Williams, 186

Okeghem, Jean d', 21

Oliver Cromwell is Buried and
Dead, Britten, 187

O Mort, poussière d'étoiles (Oh
Death, Dust of the Stars),
Fauré, 132

On a Balcony by the Sea,
Sibelius, 181

On Watch, Shostakovich, 171

On Wenlock Edge, Vaughn
Williams, 186

Orff, Carl, 19
Carmina Burana, 19

Oriental Romance, Glazunov, 167

Our Youth, Rorem, 193

O wüsst' ich doch den Weg
züruck (Oh, If Only I Knew
the Way Back), Brahms, 86,
88–9

P

Pantomime, Debussy, 141

Paradis, Fauré, 132

Pastorale des petits cochons roses
(Pastoral of the Little Pink
Pigs), Chabrier, 151

Pedrell, Felipe, 173

Pelléas et Mélisande, Debussy,
141, 144

Pergolesi, Giovanni, 70

Peri, Jacopo, 22

Persian Songs, Rubinstein, 167

Peter Grimes, Britten, 186

Phydilé, Duparc, 137

Pierrot-Lunaire, Schoenberg, 111,
114, 115–7, 190

Please Don't Go, Rachmaninov,
168

Poema en forma de canciones
(Poem in form of a Song),
Turina, 175

Poemè d'un jour (Poem of One
Day), Fauré, 129

Poèmes juifs (Jewish Poems),
Milhaud, 156

Poems by Anna Akhmatova,
Prokofiev, 169

Poems of Love and the Rain,
Rorem, 193

Polo, Falla, 195

Poppies in July, Rorem, 192–3

Poulenc, Francis, 149, 151, 155,
157–8, 196
Avant le cinéma, 158

Banalités, 158
C'est le joli printemps, 157
Chanson de la fille frivole, 157
Chansons gaillardes, 158
Chansons villageoises, 157–8
Dialogues des Carmélites, 157
Gloria, 157
Hotel, 158
Hymne, 158
Le Bestiaire, 151
Les Gars qui vont à la fête, 157
Le Mendiant, 157
Le Souris, 158
Sanglots, 158
Pride, Borodin, 162
Pride, Moussorgsky, 165
The Princess, Grieg, 177
Prison, Fauré, 130
The Prison, Shostakovich, 171
Prodigal Son, Britten, 186
Prokofiev, Sergei, 169
Five Songs Without Words, 169
Poems by Anna Akhmatova, 169
Three Romances, 169
The Ugly Duckling, 169
Proses lyriques, Debussy, 142
Purcell, Henry, 22, 26–8, 35, 182, 185, 187
The Blessed Virgin's Expostulation, 27
Choice Ayres, 26
Dido and Aneas, 26–7
The Fatal Hour Comes on Apace, 27
If Music be the Food of Love, 27
I Love and I Must, 27–8
Not All My Torments, 27–8
Upon a Quiet Conscience, 27–8

Q

Quand tu chantes (When You Sing), Berlioz, 123

Quatres Chansons populaires (Four Popular Songs), Ravel, 151

R

Rachmaninov, Sergei, 14, 160, 166, 167–8
Christ is Risen, 168
The Harvest of Sorrow, 168
In the Silence of the Night, 168
Lilacs, 168
Oh, Do Not Grieve, 168
Oh, Never Sing to Me Again, 167
Please Don't Go, 168
The Storm, 168
To the Children, 168
Vocalise, 168
Radiant Night, Grieg, 177
Ragnheld, Grieg, 177
Rameau, Jean Philippe, 120
Ravel, Maurice, 14, 121, 128, 149–153, 154, 159, 175
Chanson à boire, 153
Chanson épique, 153
Chanson romanesque, 153
Chansons madécasses, 14, 152–3
Cinq mélodies grèques populaires, 151
Deux Mélodies hebraïques, 151
Don Quichotte à Dulcinée, 153
Histoires naturelles, 150
Quatres Chansons populaires, 151
Shéhérazade, 149–50
Vocalise en forme d'habanera, 150
Reger, Max, 91
Rencontre (Meeting), Fauré, 129
Requiem, Brahms, 87
Rhapsodie, Weber, 56
Reichardt, Johann, 55

Der Erlkönig, 55
Reiselied (Traveling Song),
    Mendelssohn, 82–3
Rimsky–Korsakov, Nicolai,
    164–5, 173
Rodrigo, Joaquin, 176
    Canciones sobre textos
        castillanos, 176
    Madrigales amatorios, 176
Rorem, Ned, 192–3
    Ariel, 192
    Lady Lazarus, 193
    Last Poems of Wallace Stevens,
        193
    Love's Stricken "Why", 193
    Our Youth, 193
    Poems of Love and the Rain,
        193
    Poppies in July, 192–3
    This is the House of Bedlam,
        192
Roses ardentes, Fauré, 132
Roussel, Albert, 153
Rubinstein, Anton, 167
    Night, 167
    Persian Songs, 167
Russlan and Ludmila, Glinka, 161

S

Salieri, Antonio, 49
Sally Gardens, Britten, 187
Salome, Strauss, 104
Samson, Händel, 29
Sanglots (Sighs), Poulenc, 158
Sappho's Love Song, Kodály, 180
Satie, Erik, 149, 153–5
    Socrate, 155
Scarlatti, Alessandro, 23–6
    O Cessate di Piagarmi, 25
    Se Florindo è fedele, 24–5
    Spesso vibra per suo gioco, 25
Scarlatti, Domenico, 23, 159
Schilflied (Reed Song),

Mendelssohn, 83
Schliesse mir die Augen beide
    (Close My Eyes), Berg,
    118–120
Schoenberg, Arnold, 57, 110–120,
    167, 190
    Dank, 111
    Das Buch der hängenden
        Gärten, 110, 113–5
    Erwartung, 112, 115
    Four Songs with Orchestra, 117
    Jesus Bettelt, 112
    Kol Nidrei, 118
    Moses und Aron, 118
    Ode to Napoleon, 118
    Pierrot-Lunaire, 111, 114,
        115–7, 190
    Sommermüd, 110
    A Survivor from Warsaw, 118
    Von Heute auf Morgan, 118
    Waldsonne, 112–3
Schubert, Franz, 13, 22, 43, 48,
    55, 57, 58–71, 72, 79, 84, 85,
    86, 94, 102, 121, 178
    An die Musik, 59
    Auf dem Wasser zu singen, 59,
        62–3
    Der Doppelgänger, 59, 69
    Der Erlkönig, 55, 59, 61–3, 67
    Der greise Kopf, 65
    Der Hirt auf dem Felsen, 14,
        55, 59, 70–1
    Der Leiermann, 59, 67–8
    Der Lindenbaum, 59, 65, 79–80
    Der Tod und das Mädchen, 59
    Der Wanderer, 59
    Der Wegweiser, 67
    Die Forelle, 59, 62
    Die Krähe, 67
    Die Liebe liebt das Wandern, 65
    Die Post, 59, 66–7
    Die schöne Mullerin, 59, 63–4
    Einsamkeit, 65

Erstarrung, 65
Ganymed, 59
Gefor'ne Thränen, 65
Gretchen am Spinnrade, 43,
    59–61
Heidenröslein, 59
Nun ist die Welt so trübe, 65
Schwanengesang, 68
Ständchen, 59, 68–9
Täuschung, 65
Winterreise, 59, 63, 65
Wohin? 59, 64–5
Schulz, Johann, 55
Schumann, Robert, 22, 71–80,
    84–5, 86–7, 89, 92, 93–4, 102,
    121, 195
An meinem Herzen, an meiner
    Brust, 77
Der Nussbaum, 73, 79–80, 89
Dichterliebe, 72, 73, 195
Die beiden Grenadiere, 73, 78
Du Ring an meinem Finger, 73,
    75
Er, der Herrlichste von allen, 74
Frauenliebe und Leben, 72, 73,
    74–8
Helft mir, ihr Schwestern, 75–6
Ich kann's nicht fassen, nicht
    glauben, 75
Liederkreis, 72–3
Mondnacht, 73, 79
Myrthen, 72–3
Nun hast du mir den ersten
    Schmerz getan, 76–8
Seit ich ihn gesehn, 74
Susser Freund, 76–7
Widmung, 76
Wilhelm Meister, 72
Schwanengesang (Swan Song),
    Schubert, 68
Scriabin, Alexander, 112
Sea Drift, Delius, 183
Sea Princess, Borodin, 162

Seguidilla murciana (Seguidilla
    from Murcia), Falla, 175
Sehnsucht nach dem Frühling
    (Yearning for Spring),
    Mozart, 41–2
Se Florindo è fedele (If Florindo is
    Faithful), Scarlatti, 24–5
Seit ich ihn gesehen (Since I Have
    Seen Him), Schumann, 74
The Seminarist, Moussorgsky,
    164
Serenade, Moussorgsky, 163
Sérénade toscane (Tuscan
    Serenade), Fauré, 128
Serre d'ennui (Hothouse of
    Boredom), Chausson, 136
Serres chaudes (Hothouses),
    Chausson, 136
Se tu non lasci amore (If You Do
    Not Leave Me, My Love),
    Händel, 32–3
Seufzer (A Sigh), Wolf, 95, 98
Seven Early Songs, Berg, 118
Seven Sonnets of Michelangelo,
    Britten, 187
Seven Spanish Popular Songs,
    Falla, 175, 195
Shall a Man Spin? Moussorgsky,
    165
Sharp, Cecil, 182
Shéhérazade, Ravel, 149–150
She Never Told Her Love, Haydn,
    36–7
Shostakovich, Dimitri, 169, 170–2
Babi Yar, 170–1
Death of the Poet, 172
De Profundis, 171
Lorelei, 171
Madam, Look, 171
Malaguena, 171
O Delvig, Delvig, 172
On Watch, 171
The Prison, 171

The Suicide, 171
Sibelius, Jean, 178, 180–1
  Black Roses, 181
  Come Away Death, 181
  The First Kiss, 181
  In a Balcony by the Sea, 181
  Spring Flies Fast, 181
  The Tryst, 181
The Side Show, Ives, 190
Six Medieval Lyrics, Holst, 186
Sixteen Songs for Children,
    Tchaikovsky, 167
Slavonic Mass, Janáček, 178
Sleeping Beauty, Borodin, 162
Sleep is Supposed to Be, Copland,
    192
Smetena, Bedřich, 177
Socrate, Satie, 155
Softly the Spirit Flew Up to
    Heaven, Moussorgsky, 165
Sommermüd (Summer Mood),
    Schoenberg, 110
Songs and Dances of Death,
    Moussorgsky, 163
Songs and Proverbs of William
    Blake, Britten, 187
Songs from the Norwegian,
    Delius, 182
Songs My Mother Taught Me,
    Dvořák, 178
Songs of Travel, Vaughn
    Williams, 184–5
The Sound of Autumn, Bartók,
    180
Soupir (Sigh), Duparc, 137–9
Spanisches Liederbuch (Spanish
    Songbook), Wolf, 93, 98–9
Spesso vibra per suo gioco (Oft
    the Blindfold Boy), Scarlatti,
    25
The Spirit's Song, Haydn, 36,
    39–40
Spleen, Fauré, 130

Spohr, Louis, 55
  German Songs, 55
  Wiegenlied, 56
  Zwiegesang, 56
Spring Flies Fast, Sibelius, 181
Springtime, Grieg, 177
Ständchen (Serenade), Schubert,
    59, 68–9
Ständchen, Strauss, 107
The Stone Guest, Dargomizhsky,
    161
The Storm, Rachmaninov, 168
Stradella, Alessandro, 23, 26
Strauss, Richard, 58, 92,
    102–109, 111
  Ariadne auf Naxos, 104, 109
  Der Rosenkavalier, 104, 109
  Elektra, 104
  Heimliche Aufforderung, 105,
      109
  Mein Herz ist stumm, 105,
      108–9
  Salome, 104
  Ständchen, 107
  Wie sollten wir geheim sie
      halten? 105, 108
  Zeitlose, 105–7
Stravinsky, Igor, 167, 169
The Suicide, Shostakovich, 171
Sur les lagunes (On the Lagoons),
    Berlioz, 122
A Survivor from Warsaw,
    Schoenberg, 118
Susser Freund (Sweet Friend),
    Schumann, 76–7

T

Tailleferre, Germaine, 155
Täuschung (Illusion), Schubert,
    65
Tchaikovsky, Peter Illich, 160,
    165–7
  Again, as Before, Alone, 167

Does the Day Dawn, 166
Had I Only Known, 166
Sixteen Songs for Children, 167
Was I Not a Blade of Grass, 166
Testament, Duparc, 137
There Came a Wind Like A Bugle, Copland, 191
They Are There, Ives, 190
The Things our Fathers Loved, Ives, 190
This is the House of Bedlam, Rorem, 192
Thou Hast Made Me, Britten, 187
Three Verlaine Songs, Delius, 183
Tom Sails Away, Ives, 190
To the Children, Rachmaninov, 168
Three Romances, Prokofiev, 169
Tonadillas al Estilo Antiguo (Tonadillas in Antique Style), Granados, 173–4
Toujours (Always), Fauré, 129–130
Trennungslied (Song of Leaving), Mozart, 44
Trepak, Moussorgsky, 163
Treue Liebe (True Love), Brahms, 86–7
Trois Ballades de François Villon (Three Ballads of François Villon), Debussy, 142
Trois Mélodies (Three Melodies), Falla, 174
The Tryst, Sibelius, 181
Turina, Joaquin, 175–6
  Canto a Sevilla, 176
  Dedication, 175
  Dos canciones, 175
  Las Locas por amor, 175
  Poema en forma de conciones, 175
  Vocalizaciones, 175
Two Little Flowers, Ives, 190

U

The Ugly Duckling, Prokofiev, 169
Um Mitternacht (At Midnight), Wolf, 95–6
Upon a Quiet Conscience, Purcell, 27–8

V

Vaughn Williams, Ralph, 14, 184–6
  Antiphon, 185
  Bredon Hall, 186
  The Call, 185
  Five Mystical Songs, 185
  Greensleeves, 184
  I Got Me Flowers, 185
  Is My Team Ploughing? 186
  Let Beauty Awake, 185
  Linda Lea, 184
  Oh, When I Was in Love with You, 186
  On Wenlock Edge, 186
  Songs of Travel, 184–5
  Youth and Love, 185
Venise, Gounod, 123
Vier ernste Gesänge (Four Serious Songs), Brahms, 85–6
Villanelle des petits canards (Villanelle of the Little Ducks), Chabrier, 151
Vocalise, Rachmaninov, 168
Vocalise en forme d'habanera, Ravel, 150
Vocalizaciones, Turina, 175
Voici que le printemps (Here is Spring), Debussy, 141
Volkslied (Folk Song), Mendelssohn, 84
Von Heute auf Morgen (From Today till Tomorrow), Schoenberg, 118

Vous ne priez pas (You Are Not Praying), Bizet, 124–5

W

Wagner, Richard, 76, 94, 95, 102–3, 111, 182
Waldsonne (Forest Sun), Schoenberg, 112–3
Was I Not a Blade of Grass, Tchaikovsky, 166
Weber, Karl Maria von, 55, 56, 57
Der Freischütz, 56
Oberon, 56
Rhapsodie, 56
Webern, Anton von, 118
Wedding March, Mendelssohn, 135
When General William Booth Enters Into Heaven, Ives, 189
When They Come Back, Copland, 192
Why Do They Shut Me Out of Heaven? Copland, 191
Widmung (Dedication), Schumann, 76
Wiegenlied (Lullaby), Spohr, 56
Wie lange schon (How Long It's Been), Wolf, 95, 101
Wie sollten wir geheim sie halten (How Can We Keep Secret?), Strauss, 105, 108
Wilhelm Meister, Schumann, 72
Winterreise (Winter's Journey), Schubert, 59, 63, 65
Wir haben beide lange Zeit geschwiegen (In Silence Each the Other Passed), Wolf, 95, 101
With a Water Lily, Grieg, 177
Wohin? (Where), Schubert, 59, 64–5
Wolf, Hugo, 58, 91, 92–101, 102
Begegnung, 95–6

Das verlassene Mägdlein, 95–7
Der Corregidor, 94
Die ihr schwebet um diese Palmen, 95, 98
Elfenlied, 95, 97–8
Geh', Geliebter, geh' jetzt, 93, 99
Italienisches Liederbuch, 93, 95, 100
Liede vom Winde, 97
Manuel Venegas, 94
Mein Liebster singt, 95, 101
Nixe Binefuss, 97
Seufzer, 95, 98
Spanisches Liederbuch, 93, 98–9
Um Mitternacht, 95–6
Wie Lange schon, 95, 101
Wir haben beide lange Zeit geschwiegen, 95, 101
Woodland Wandering, Grieg, 177
The World Feels Dusty, Copland, 192
Wozzeck, Berg, 118

Y

You Drunken Sot, Moussorgsky, 164
Youth and Love, Vaughan Williams, 185

Z

Zaïde, Berlioz, 123
Zeitlose (The Saffron), Strauss, 105–7
Zelter, Karl Friedrich, 55
Der Erlkönig, 55
Zumsteeg, Johann, 55
Zweistimmige Lieder (Songs for Two Voices), Mendelssohn, 84
Zwiegesang (Two Songs in One), Spohr, 56